LIFE UPON THE WICKED STAGE

Clipper Studies in the Theatre
ISSN 0748-237X
Number Fourteen

Life
upon the
Wicked Stage

*A Visit to the American Theatre
of the 1860s, 1870s, and 1880s As Seen
in the Pages of the New York Clipper*

Edited by

William L. Slout

BORGO PRESS / WILDSIDE PRESS

www.wildsidepress.com

*   *   *   *   *   *   *   *

Library of Congress Cataloging-in-Publication Data

Life upon the wicked stage : a visit to the American theatre of the 1860s,
1870s, and 1880s as seen in the pages of New York clipper / edited by
William L. Slout.
    p. cm. — (Clipper studies in the theatre, ISSN 0748-237X ; no. 14)
Includes index.
    ISBN 0-89370-363-X (cloth). — ISBN 0-89370-463-6 (pbk.)
    1. Theater—United States—History—19th century. I. Slout, William L.
(William Lawrence) II. New York clipper. III. Series.
PN2259.L54 1996   96-1562
792'.0973'09034—dc20   CIP

FIRST EDITION

CONTENTS

PART IV: ABOUT PERFORMANCE

PART V: ABOUT THEATRICAL PROMOTION

PART VI: ABOUT THE MUSICAL STAGE, ETC.

ILLUSTRATIONS

Page x: The character of Lord Dundreary in Tom Taylor's history making "Our American Cousin." New York, 1858.

Page xii: "The-Ticket-of-Leave-Man," Act IV, Scene 1. Detective Hawkshaw reveals his identity to Bob Brierly, the ticket-of-leave-man. New York, 1863.

Page 4: Act I in "True To The Core; A Story Of The Armada" the beacon is lighted by Marah, the Gypsy girl. New York, 1866.

Page 10: Mary has fainted at the arrival of Rawdon Scudamore, her first husband, in Act I of "Hunted Down; or, The Two Lives Of Mary Leigh." New York, 1869.

Page 14: A village churchyard in Austria, the setting for Act IV, Scene 3, of Augustin Daly's "Leah, The Forsaken." New York, 1863.

Page 30: Laura Courtland breaks out of the shed in which she has been confined to save an anxious Joe Snorkey from discomfort in Act III, Scene 3, of the classic, "Under The Gaslight."

Page 38: The stage Irishman.

Page 42: The deck of the *Lively Polly*, an illustration for Henry Brougham Farnie's "Sinbad The Sailor; or, The Ungenial Genie And The Cabin Boy." New York, 1869.

Page 82: A set-to in the thieve's cellar, Act III, of press agent Charles Gayler's "The Child Stealer." New York, 1866.

Page 92: Lady Audley is discovered in Act I of "Lady Audley's Secret" pushing her first husband, George Talboys, into a well. New York, 1863.

Page 104: Thinking Ferne has avowed love for her out of pity, Eva has attempted to take her life by walking out into the cold and snow in Act II of "Progress." New York, 1869.

Page 112: Promotion for "Divorce," taken from Anthony Trollope's *He Knew He Was Right*. New York, 1871.

PREFACE

The American theatre underwent marked changes in the years following the Civil War. With the conflict out of the way, the country settled into a period of physical and financial growth which was reflected in the business of amusement as well.

Rail mileage was increased everywhere. In the South, railroad activity in the years immediately after 1865 constituted the rehabilitation of facilities damaged in the war. Then an outburst of construction, financed by Northern and European capital, got under way and by 1890 the South had increased its trackage from 9,000 to 50,000 miles.

Concurrently, railroad building moved westward, epitomized by the great transcontinental lines. The idea of a transcontinental road--one that would extend from a point in the Mississippi Valley to the Pacific coast--had been discussed before the war. Then, Congress moved to make the idea a reality by passing an act in 1862 and amending it in 1864, which chartered two railroad corporations, the Union Pacific and the Central Pacific. The Union Pacific was to build westward from Omaha, Nebraska, and the Central Pacific eastward from Sacramento, California, until they met at the eastern boundary of California. Work started in 1865. An incentive to fast building was added when the Central Pacific was given permission to lay track beyond California, thus making the project a horrendous race between the two corporations. The competitors met on May 10, 1869, when the last rails of the Union Pacific and the Central Pacific were joined at Promontory Point, Utah.

The steel umbilical linking East and West opened the way for a rush of theatrical activity. New cities and towns were born, wherein, in no time, new theatre structures were erected. Such growth was inviting to prospective impresarios, who formed traveling companies to entertain the audiences ready and waiting for new diversions.

By this time the native American actors were well established. Edwin Booth and others of the "classic school" were setting the pattern away from the heroic histrionics of past years and laying a foundation for realism to match the changing images on the physical stage. With the emergence of native stars, the combination system, the practice of a leading actor touring with a complete production as opposed to the old system of the star moving alone from one stock company to another, was created. This allowed plays and other theatrical genre to book into places that had theatres but no standing resident supporting players.

Spectacle and scenic realism had become visually exciting and, for its time, astonishingly lifelike. The box set was beginning to replace the traditional wings and drops, and three dimensional elements were usurping the painter's art. New mechanical devices were developed for creating more rapid scene changes. And electrical installations were supplanting gas jets, giving greater control and flexibility in illuminating the stage.

The choice of stage offerings were on their way to becoming greater and more varied than had ever been available to American audiences. Variety entertainment was emerging from the squalid concert saloons and moving toward a family oriented fare, abetted by the father of the vaudeville stage, Tony Pastor. The amazing success in 1866 of the musical spectacle, "The Black Crook," bred scores of imitators. And such perennial attractions as minstrelsy and "Uncle Tom's Cabin" companies now followed the rail lines to most every nook and cranny of the country.

Theatre management was turning into big business. Strong and resourceful operators, able to envision unified productions and the means of making them enticing to a larger share of the populous, had entered the field. More lavish techniques of promotion were created in the wake of the P. T. Barnum "ballywagon." Newspapers were becoming more and more responsive to stage events. Hence, enter the press agent. And with the founding of the *New York Clipper*, detailed theatrical news was made available to professionals and the public alike. Yet for all this, the theatre of this period, before and behind the scenes, remains a mystery to many Americans.

The articles that form this volume are compiled from the pages of the *New York Clipper*. Covering a period within the 1860s, 1870s, and 1880s, they are representative of a naive sentiment regarding the theatre of that day, self-conscious and protective, sensitive toward outside pressures and puritanical abuses, and self-critical of personal behavior within the little world of theatrical troupes.

The *Clipper* was first published on April 30, 1853, by Harrison Fulton Trent to serve as a sporting weekly. It carried news items concerned with such athletic activities as sailing, baseball, prize fighting, and pedestrianism. The paper was sold to Frank Queen in 1855, who, as sole proprietor and editor, soon established it as the major organ with an international readership and a reputation for reliability. Following this change of management, the paper began including theatrical news, which increased in emphasis during the 1860's when war necessitated the shutting down of the *Spirit of the Times* because of its large circulation in the South. Practically speaking, the *Clipper* was the sole theatrical paper in America during the decade of 1865-1875; and by the end of the century it was the most complete weekly chronicler of the amusement business. It continued to be until competition from *Billboard* and *Variety* forced its demise in 1924.

Under Queen's guiding force the *Clipper* befriended the popular amusements neglected by the other publications. In addition to its dramatic interests, it became the major source for circus, minstrel and variety news, a position it held throughout the century. When vaudeville evolved from the old variety performances, the *Clipper* responded by becoming the journalistic organ for it, aiding in its development from variety hall and concert saloon origins to its eventual popular and respected position in the entertainment world. Through active exploitation of the circus, minstrelsy and vaudeville, the *Clipper* became known to those who were a part of these branches of the business as "The Old Reliable" and "The Showman's Bible."

Like most of the weeklies of its day, the *Clipper* used staff writers as well as accepting material from free-lancers and occasional contributors, most of whom wrote under pseudonyms or complete anonymity. One should assume then that the contributions in this volume were authored by both journalists and theatrical professionals. Their total offerings herein gathered combine to display a canvas of theatrical activity, in color, texture, and mood, occurring in the latter half of the nineteenth century.

The reader should be aware that aforementioned have been occasionally edited to correct typesetting errors and to make sometimes cumbersome syntax more readable.

William L. Slout, editor

Life Upon
The Wicked Stage

A Visit to the American Theatre
of the 1860s, 1870s, and 1880s, as Seen in the Pages
of the *New York Clipper*

PART I: ABOUT THEATRE PEOPLE

✤

A LITTLE GOSSIP ABOUT SHOW PEOPLE
by Ralph Keeler

In his social relations a performer, like many another great man or woman, is liable to mistakes of head and heart. It is a pretty generally known fact, for instance, that the most famous tenor of our day is so careful of his gloves as to fly into a towering rage with any lady who touches them with more than her fingertips in the most impassioned duets. And a very celebrated *prima donna*, who takes the world captive as much by the exceeding loveliness of her person and manner as by her wonderful voice, is in the habit of beating her maid abominably two or three times a week. It would, indeed, be an acute analysis which should determine just what it is in the higher walks of music that makes the lives of its special votaries so strikingly inharmonious. He or she who has known of an operatic company wherein the four leading persons were on speaking terms with one another, off the stage, has known a remarkable fact in the history of that peculiar class. Of these, and of the dramatic profession proper, I would perhaps have no right to speak here, were it not for the fact that, in my time at least, there was a sort of fraternity among all people who appeared before the footlights. I do not know whether the members of cork opera associate with the better class of actors at this day, but I think they do not. I would venture to assert, however, that among the lower orders of actors, minstrels and circus riders, there ever will be such a spirit of Bohemianism--such a touch of hearty, reckless good nature--as will always make their whole world kin.

Jealousy may be set down as the chief failing of the whole race, high or low. I have known men, whose names have made some noise in the world, to measure with straws the comparative sizes of the letters in which they were announced on a poster. But among minstrels, especially, a thorough worldliness and boon companionship enable them generally to be civil to one another, whatsoever their private feelings.

An old showman at last comes to look upon the quiet ways of ordinary life with that same kind of longing, romantic interest with which a certain species of imaginative youth are always looking upon the impossible glory of traveling with a show. A droll sighing for rural pursuits seems to be the most common form taken by the romance of your veteran itinerant. Yet, oddly enough, there is scarce any one whom he holds personally in such ridiculous contempt as he does the honest farmer. The vow which the old sailor in the forecastle is forever making to go to sea no more is rarely remembered over three days on land. And so it is with the cognate ideal which floats in the queer imagination of the old showman. I never knew but three or four who attained anything like the realization of their romantic purpose. Daniel Emmett, the author of many of the best known of the earlier Negro melodies, did so far reach the fleeting object of his bucolic ambition as to have a large, well filled chicken coop in the back yard of a rented house in the suburbs of a great city.

The ladies of the profession are sometimes given to gossip and backbiting in as great a degree at least as are the gentlemen. Jealousy may be as rife on a Mississippi showboat as in the ante-chamber of any court in Europe. I have known a *danseuse* to furnish boys with clandestine bouquets to throw on the stage when she appeared; not that she cared at all for the praise or blame of the audience, but that she did care to crush a cleverer rival.

In our company on board the *Palace* and the *Raymond* (the famous river showboats), we had strange contrasts in human nature. It would happen, for instance, that the man who could not sleep without snoring would be placed in the same stateroom with the man who could not sleep within hearing of the most distant snore. The man who could not eat pork was seated at table just opposite the man who doted on it. We had one gentleman--the fleshy bass singer already mentioned--who spent all his leisure in catching mocking birds; and another, who passed his spare hours in contriving new and undiscoverable ways of letting these birds escape from the cages. There were on board ladies who had seen more prosperous days, when they were the chief attraction at the theatres of London, Paris and New York--according to their own stories; other ladies who had never associated with such vulgar people before; other ladies who hoped they would die if they did not leave the company at the very next landing, but never left; and yet other ladies, I am rejoiced to add, who were lovely in nature and deed--kind mothers and faithful wives, whose strength of character and ready cheerfulness tended as far as possible to restore the social equilibrium.

In the course of the long association, grotesque friendships sprang up. The man who played the bass drum was the bosom companion of the man who had charge of the machine for making the gas which supplied the two boats. The pretty man of the establishment, he who played the chimes on the top of the museum and the piano in the concert room--at present a popular composer at St. Louis--this young gentleman, who broke all the hearts of the country girls that came into the show, was the inseparable friend of the pilot--a great, gruff, warm hearted fellow, who steered the *Raymond* from the corners of his eyes and swore terribly at snags. The man who dusted down Tam O'Shanter and the Twelve Apostles in wax, and had especial care of the stuffed birds, giraffes and alligators, was on most intimate terms with the cook.

As a general thing the ladies, performers and crew of our boats were not so quarrelsome as I have seen a set of cabin passengers on a sea voyage between America and Europe, or especially on the three weeks' passage to or from California. When I consider that there were so many of us together in this narrow compass for nearly a year, it seems to me strange indeed that there was not more bad blood excited.

Mme. Olinza was, I believe, the name of the Polish lady who walked on a tight-rope from the floor of one end of the Museum up to the roof of the farthest gallery. This kind of perilous ascension and suspension was something new in the country then. It was before the time of Blondin, and Madame used to produce a great sensation. Now it may be interesting to the general reader to learn that this tight-rope walker was one of the most exemplary, domestic little bodies imaginable. She and her husband had a large stateroom on the upper deck of the *Raymond*, and she was always there with her child when released from her public duties. One afternoon the nurse happened to bring the child into the Museum when Mme. Olinza was on the rope; and out of the vast audience that little face was recognized by its fond mother and her attention so distracted that she lost her balance, dropped her pole, and fell. Catching the rope with her hands, however, in time to break her

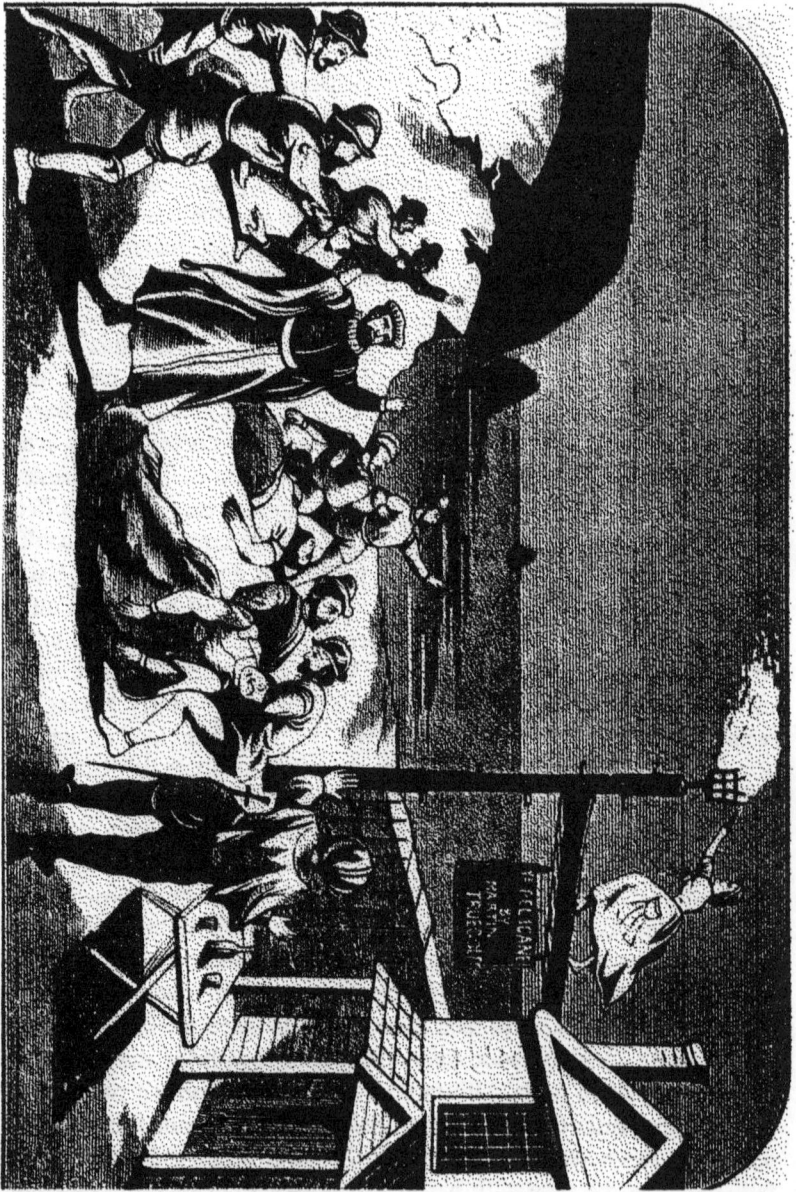

fall, she escaped, fortunately, without the least injury; but ever after that her child was kept out of the audience while she was on the rope.

[*New York Clipper*, November 19, 1870]

THE STAGE GRUMBLER
by Marcus Moriarty

Very nearly every theatre we find tinctured with this odious pest. In fact, we are all more or less possessed with a tendency to grumble. Why such is the case, we leave to moralists and philosophers to determine. We merely take the fact as we find it.

The only effectual way of resisting the temptation of becoming a stage grumbler is to observe how odious it is to others, how the stage grumbler is the subject of pity and contempt--pity that a person, amiable in other respects, cannot comprehend that he is merely an individual, and that the little world in which he exists is not depending on him or his opinions, and that it could get along just as well if he had never existed, and that when he leaves a company a sigh of relief will be the result.

It would seem that the grumbler is profoundly impressed with the idea that he is one of Heaven's persecuted angels. He is, in most cases, an egotist, and deems that he alone is capable of becoming proficient in his profession. Who has not been disgusted--nay, even driven almost to desperation--by the incessant hissing in his ears of "I'll not play this part," "I'll not do this or that"? And yet this grumbler will probably do the very thing he has so vehemently declared he would not do. Why, the "chills" is but a gentle soothing movement of the body when compared with the grating and rasping the nerves must endure from the perpetual grumbling of this little "I won't." He cannot be silenced, even in open controversy; or, if he is, it will be to grumble under his breath. Logical reasoning, cogent argument, proofs bright as the noonday sun, are not so weighty as a feather in the balance against him. He is determined to grumble and no reasoning can persuade him to do otherwise.

We find him giving advice to his superiors, reproving his betters, and using harsh words to his equals. The little failings--and who has them not?--of his actors and actresses are, when he is not grumbling, magnified and made the subject of conversation; while on the other hand, the good qualities that the censured one may possess are carefully kept out of sight. If any of his companions have been so unfortunate as to have swerved from the path of duty, or to have made any slight blunder during a performance, he makes it his duty to tell everyone he sees, and he goes to a great deal of trouble to see a great many. These are examples of actors and actresses, formerly amiable and deserving in every other respect, who, becoming addicted to this disagreeable habit, gradually fall from their enviable position and became a scorn to their profession.

The grumbler can be easily pointed out in a company, because he has about him a mean, hang-dog look that tempts everybody else to grumble at him. To managers he grumbles about his companions, and then grumbles to his companions about his manager. He grumbles at an actor or actress because neither does certain things, and then grumbles if either does those very things. If he should see a companion striving to advance himself in the profession, the grumbler is sure to ascribe bad motives to him; and if the same person, through thoughtlessness or forgetfulness, should neglect some very slight duty, this miserable man is sure to grumble. The sooner a company is rid of such an individual, the better for the company; because he is never happy himself and renders unhappy all those with whom he is connected.

[*New York Clipper*, July 18, 1874]

THE ACTOR
by Bambrino

The dramatic production may be compared to a grand lottery in which a certain number of players are winners. Many an actor plods on through half his lifetime without scarcely making a "hit" worth mentioning, when all at once, at a sudden revolution of the wheel of fortune, he perhaps strikes upon some character that hits the public immensely and makes him famous and places him on the road to fortune and renown. Many, though, go their weary way till the final curtain falls upon them, never during their theatrical career having drawn the ghost of a prize. Others again, more fortunate than they, draw half prizes and quarters and sixteenths in the dramatic lottery, and retire on a moderate competence at last to that haven, the heart's desire of thousands of players, a "country place." The progress of enlightenment that goes steadily on has worked wonders for the actor as well as his fellow men. "Vagabond" is no longer written against his name, nor is he now regarded as an outcast from society, nor does he beg for patronage and play for a base pittance in barns and booths as of yore; but, instead, takes his stand as the member of an honorable profession, in which (as we have said) he may often win fortune and renown.

But the prejudice against "the players" of two hundred years ago still lingers on the earth. Twin sister of ignorance, prejudice, clings on with great tenacity and gives vent to denunciations against the actor through the medium of the bigoted and narrow minded aspersions that may wound the actor's pride, but cannot hurt him otherwise. For the public, who as a mass, side with him and cheer and encourage him, bears witness how seldom the actor appears before the bar of justice in the role of a great criminal, and how little malice he bears in his heart against even his detractors, since he returns good for evil and plays annually, in the city of New York at least, gratis, for the benefit of a society whose ministers too often cry down his profession from their pulpits.

The actor being a public character, whatever he says or does, if he holds any position of note in his profession, is peculiarly interesting to a certain morbidly inquisitive class of people; and the tenor of his private life is pried into by such most unmercifully. Indeed, his little failings off the stage are criticized more severely than are his shortcomings on the stage; and any misdemeanor that might escape notice, being the act of a private individual, seldom fails to be heralded forth if committed by a member of the dramatic profession; for the actor, in a measure at least, seems to be public property. A private individual, having indulged too freely over his wine, may take his after dinner nap and sleep off the effects with no visions of an expectant public nor the hands of the clock remorselessly pointing towards "seven." But the actor who may have indulged too freely has such visions and must rouse himself and face the public somehow, for he is their servant. And should he unfortunately betray his condition when he gets upon the stage--well, we all know pretty well the penalty that awaits him then, and the second penalty that awaits him (if the fates are against him) in the next morning's critique. And he knows to his own sorrow the third penalty awaiting him when he shall encounter the stage manager. It would be against all reason and useless to attempt to defend any man for appearing before an audience in an intoxicated condition; for a drunken performer not only insults his audience by appearing before them in such a state, but often not only ruins his own performance but distresses his fellow actors and damns the play. But there is, from time to time, such a hue and cry raised about the prevalence of drinking among the members of the theatre, that if an actor be really ill and unable to perform, the apology made for him is, in nine cases out of ten, received by an audience in a doubtful manner; knowing looks are interchanged, and at that fatal word "indisposed"—which has become one of sneering significance when applied to an actor--smiles may be detected in the auditorium. Now we wish to quote a passage from an article written by Dr. B. W. Richardson, which may explain (if not excuse) the use of stimulants by a dramatic artist.

"The dramatic artist differs from the classes previously mentioned--authors and painters--both in his labors and in his sufferings. To men of strong build and firm will, to men who possess by nature the very faculties which they represent, dramatic art may offer few anxieties or perils; and we know from experience that some of our greatest dramatists have passed through their active careers, extending over a long life, without suffering beyond other men. But if my experience serves me rightly, the majority of players are very differently placed. A man in the studio can labor at works of art calmly and quietly, thinking, as he touches the inanimate canvas, of what will be said of the result; but that is very different from the art in which the man transforms his own body into art, and has to appear suddenly before a crowd, exhibiting himself in attitude and character, personifying what he has never seen. To get up to this ordeal, interest, labor and presence of mind are required, the strongest will and the most refined ideal. We have an illustration of this intensity in those cases common, I believe, to almost every player, when the artist, at his first appearance, is said to be "stage struck" when, for the moment, the circulation stands still, when the muscles are rigid and the face deathly. This is the first and probably the most painful ordeal. But it is an ordeal which rarely ceases altogether with the first appearance. Without manifesting itself with the same active symptoms as those that are combined at the "stage struck" period, it exhibits itself in a nervous, irritable excitement, which intensifies up to the period when the time arrives for taking part in the proceedings, and then gradually subsides during the performance, or is even transformed into enthusiasm, to be followed, when the excitement is over, by a depression that may even amount to despair; a depression which applause and admiration do not satisfy, but which unjust and unfair criticism goads either into melancholy or apathy. Under these influences many of our very best players sink into second and third positions; not because they are wanting in the talent to stand first, but for the simple reason that they prefer the ease of mediocrity. For this reason some of our players who do stand first, owing to the constant irritation to which they are subjected, become cross, irritable, and despondent, finding no satisfaction in the temporary approbation which they achieve, but overwhelming chagrin at every shade of disappointment. Still more, in the very act of the sustaining of certain characters on the stage, telling physical efforts are called forth which demand a degree of muscular exertion, mental strain, and expenditure of vital force, altogether of which the mere looker-on has no adequate conception.

Take the play of "Othello," for instance, as indicating the character of the labor that is required in the actor. The mere effort of speaking such a play well is beyond the reach of ninety-nine men out of a hundred, and then add to the speech the action, the studied expression, the passion--what can be more onerous, exciting and severe? The labors of the player tell mainly on the heart. That organ becomes irregular in its action; then, for a time, large and over strung, and finally degenerate, feeble and uncertain.... Whenever sensations thus excited lead the actor to resort to the use of stimulants--when without a stimulant he is unable to meet his audience or to recover from his labor--he is beginning to suffer from a second destruction, more fatal than the first."

And add to the above, trials endured by the actor, trials too often of a pecuniary nature, domestic afflictions and the hundred worldly cares and sorrows which he shares in common with all men, and then picture the amount of self control and energy requisite to banish his own emotions and anxieties and thoughts, and speak and act and laugh and smile as a totally different being. So when we witness his performance, let us call these things to mind, nor withhold the applause and encouragement that cheers him in his arduous labors, for which he so earnestly strives and deserves.

[*New York Clipper*, March 16, 1872]

CRITICISM ON ACTING BY ACTORS AND ACTRESSES

While seated in the green-room of a theatre, listening to frequent discussions on the art of acting, the criticisms by the various actors and actresses there assembled, occasionally catching the irrepressible note of self-praise faintly sounded or boldly struck, we have found that the common test applied by the majority of the members of the theatrical profession, whereby they judge the good or bad or great in acting, is comparison. In our opinion, this comparison of one player to another by the players themselves rarely yields a fair judgment; because in the theatrical profession there are woven so many personal likes and dis-likes--born of favors received or withheld, slights or insults (real and imaginary), prejudices bred by scandal, reports good and bad (false and true), with the additional strong prejudice in some cases of nationality, and a thousand other things all serving to warn or warm the feelings of an actor or actress--that nothing can be more difficult for the most im-partial critic than to compare with strict impartiality.

Take for instance the common discussion in the green-room on the correct impersonation of the character of Hamlet. One actor will perhaps assert that Mr. Edwin Booth is the only great Hamlet he ever saw and that he has seen many. Another may vehemently declare that Mr. Edwin Forrest was the best Hamlet the world ever saw. Others, perhaps, proclaim like distinction for Macready, Barry Sullivan, Gustavus Brooke, Lawrence Barrett, Davenport or our latest representative, John McCullough, and so on through the list of known impersonators of that character. The discussion will inevitably grow warm on the respective merits of the above named players and they will inevitably be compared one with another.

We may presume that nearly every actor or actress taking part in this discussion has at some time acted with one or another of the par-ties named, and in the discussion they will insensibly allow their per-sonal likes or dislikes to influence their criticism and elevate one Hamlet to the disparagement of another Hamlet. Would this be a just criticism on the individual merits of those actors in the character of Hamlet?

Take another supposition case of a green-room discussion on Hamlet, where all assembled have seen but one actor, one and the same, play the part, and that none present have ever played the part. In criti-cizing the performance of Hamlet they cannot, therefore, compare it with that of any other actor except by hearsay; and to judge whether his assumption was a correct one they would undoubtedly advance their individual opinion of how far he realized their ideal of Hamlet in looks, grace, or speech as the prince, the philosopher, the educated gentleman and skillful swordsman--in a word, how far he was or was not Shakespeare's Hamlet. And the presumption may safely be advanced that the verdict arrived at--whether for good or bad--would at least be more just toward the actor (if no personal like or dislike prejudiced his critics) than had they, one and all, possessed the seeming advantage of having previously witnessed the performance of others in the character.

But few actors of great merit claim that in any given character they are the best living representative of the same; and those who do so, as they challenge comparison, should be critically compared with others who have assumed the same part. The majority of actors and actresses tacitly say when playing a part, "I play this part to the best of my ability." [Thus] they should be criticized according to their ability by their fellow artists, and the praise and blame should be given with as little prejudice as a juror presumably gives his decision.

The words are often heard behind the scenes, "You should see Mr. So-and-so play the part." or "She can't play that. You should have seen Miss So-and-so or Mrs. So-and-so in it. There was acting for you." Such words are spoken without a thought of the great harm that is done in speaking them. Few, in or out of a theatre, who have not given the subject some reflection, could imagine or believe the incalculable mischief done by the too common habit of criticizing the performances of artists by comparison. The criticism too often reaches the ears at last of the person criticized and produces sometimes a most disheartening effect; and much of the heart burning, cruel, and nervous suffering endured by many in their acting, arises from a dread of this criticizing by comparison, at the hands not so much of the public as of their fellow artists.

The stage is not a bed of roses to the generality of those who tread its boards, and to plant any thorn, where thorns are already so plentiful, by the players themselves, one for another, is a cruelty too often thoughtlessly committed. There are many who criticized their fellow artists justly and dispassionately. And those who do, it is needless to say, are among our most clever artists, who have bought their cleverness by hard study and more or less hard experience, which makes them tender of the faults and loud in the praise of others whose rising ability they detect. To a few, let us hope very few, the praise of a fellow actor is as wormwood to them; and for the benefit of such we may be permitted to quote Alice Carey's lines:

> The laurel longed for, you must earn:
> It is not of the things men lend;
> And though the lesson be hard to learn,
> The sooner the better, my friend.
>
> That another's head can have your crown,
> Is a judgment all untrue;
> And to drag this man or the other down,
> Will not in the least raise you.

[New York Clipper, June 13, 1874]

THE ACTOR IN SOCIETY

When Macready determined to adopt the stage as a profession-- his father had designated him to become a lawyer--he was not, according to his own confession, aware of the distance between the two starting points in life. Many years later he wrote these words: "My experience has taught me that, whilst the law, the church, the army and navy give a man the rank of a gentleman, on the stage that designation must be obtained in society by the individual bearing." Which means, simply, that other professions confer dignity upon their followers, while the actor must earn for himself the title of gentleman in spite of his calling.

What was true in Macready's early years is true today. The actor is forced to fight against narrow-minded prejudice, and to overcome the adverse opinion of many well-meaning but bigoted people. To be received into the higher circles of society, he must attain marked distinction in his profession. Without the passport of fame his occupation condemns him. The Macreadys and Kembles and Keans of any age have enough fawning flatterers at their heels, but the rank and file of the dramatic profession are looked upon as forming a doubtful element in the complex fabric called "society."

In the early puritanical days of New England an actor was believed to be a pronounced and open servant of Satan; and the man,

woman or child who attended a theatrical performance was immediately consigned to the sulfurous regions below. Our ministers have become more considerate in these later years; and even Brother Talmage makes it possible for a player to escape the wrath to come. But while the stage is held in higher favor, and while the actor's art has come to be recognized as one worthy of patient study and liberal patronage, the members of the theatrical profession find still the barriers of prejudice shutting them out from their rightful places in society.

Every player has another part from that which he lives upon the stage. Actors are possessed of the same desires and yearnings and passions and hopes and fears which fill the breasts of other men. They cannot wholly merge their individuality into their art. They must have relaxation and pleasure like the rest of us. The heavy villain of tonight becomes a husband and father with the dawn of the morrow, and his mind is occupied with very different thoughts from those which claimed his attention in the play. The injured heroine steps from the glare of the footlights into the duties of her own domestic circle, and may be a wife and a mother for aught the public cares. In a word, our actors and actresses are but men and women. The stage does not rob them of their affections, nor blunt their sensibilities, nor make them other than human. They may assume a thousand characters, yet there remains, distinct from all these, a character of their own--modeled by the same varying influences, and bent by the same unyielding forces which mold and bend mankind the world round.

We ask for the members of the dramatic profession a broader social life. The stage itself has come down to us as one of the established institutions of civilized society. Drawing its origin from the Church, and antedating the Christian religion by hundreds of years, it is destined to exist as long as the world moves in its present orbit. Is it not fitting, then, that those who tread the boards in a professional capacity should be received as the peers of their fellow men? What superfine distinction is this which society makes between the actor's calling and that of the merchant, lawyer, doctor or priest? Shall education be made as a passport to association with the higher classes? Then look for it among the followers of the stage; you will not look in vain. Or is the barred door to be opened by the key of refinement? There are hundreds of refined men and women in theatre circles. Or is it talent that is wanted? The stage is rich in talent. Or morality? The morals of our actors will compare most favorably with those of any other class.

Let the prejudice, then, which is but a relic of bigotry and ignorance, be done away with, and let an actor be received into society as readily and as cordially as he would be if he had followed some other vocation. Not, mind you, because he is an actor; but because he is educated and refined, because his character is unstained with vice. These are the requisites demanded in others--we speak of a society founded on a truer basis than the mighty dollar--and let them be demanded likewise of the actor. If he is lacking in these qualities, he may expect to be denied admittance to the charmed circle; if he possesses them, then he has a right to demand that he shall not be ostracized because of his profession. Brown borrows dignity from his calling, which is that of a painter; Jones gives the world an early opportunity to know that he is a lawyer; the Reverend Mr. Simpkins wears a white cravat as a badge of his theological pursuits. But here is Johnson, who knows more art than Brown, as much of law as Jones, and possibly as much of religion, if not of theology, as the Reverend Mr. Simpkins; and who must live down the prejudice which exists against him because, forsooth, he is an actor. Society, in kid gloves and broadcloth, opens its arms to Brown, Jones and Simkins, not because of any personal superiority discernible in the trinity, but because of their several vocations; and this same society finds it difficult to extend a gracious hand to Johnson, whose positive virtues are overshadowed by the negative vice of his profession. And what is that profession but the embodiment, the quintessence, of all other arts? What other calling demands such preparatory schooling, such untiring devotion, such constant study and patient endeavor? As Macready well said: "In other callings the profession confers dignity upon the initiated; on the stage the player must contribute respect to the exercise of his art."

The barriers which prejudice has erected against persons connected with the stage have resulted in shutting out, to a very large degree, that intercourse with other professions which the theatre ought to enjoy. In their social lives, our actors, we think, have become too exclusive. Did they mingle more freely with men and women outside their vocation, the world would come to know that honor and virtue and sterling worth are to be found upon the stage, and that morality is not necessarily stripped off when the player's garb is donned. Learning this, the world might so far forget his prejudice as to accept a man for what he is, whether a boor in the pulpit or a gentleman upon the stage. That type of littleness, which comes only from the dignity which a profession confers, is not to be envied, after all. A pigmy may succeed in elevating himself to the castle of a giant, but his position serves only to make his littleness more conspicuous. It is not the calling that makes the man, but the man the calling. A fool is no less a fool because he pleads in court or preaches in the pulpit; and a gentleman is not one whit less a gentleman, nor a lady one whit less a lady, because they follow the profession which has produced, even in these modern days, noble men and loyal women.

[*New York Clipper*, March 3, 1877]

ACTRESSES
by Bambrino

They may be divided into three classes, *viz.*, actresses who play for money, actresses who play for their own pleasure, and actresses who play for fame. It may be set down that the majority of the actresses upon the stage play for the sake of money they earn by their professional labors, but too many only for their own pleasure and to gain notoriety and too few for fame. If a true account were written of the actress who devotes her life to the stage from an instinctive knowledge that is her "calling" and purely for love of it, what a history it would be! But we have few such histories. We have but glimpses here and there, in meager sketches and anecdotes of the lives of such, that hint to us what energy and will and honest aspiration can achieve. But few care to publish the rebuffs, the disheartening first failures, the obstacles that had to be surmounted--perhaps poverty, perhaps an ugly face, a lisp, a bad gait and figure--and the days of labor and the nights of anxiety. Ah, but we can guess at these when we recall the passage in the life of one great American actress who, failing to receive the recognition her talents deserved in her own land, sought encouragement in a distant one, where, almost friendless and unknown, by her indomitable perseverance, [she] overcame all obstacles and earned for herself a lasting renown. But "life is short and art is long" and we have but few actresses on the stage at the present day who are aspirants for enduring fame.

The rage for sensation and sensational dramas, the rapidity with which a pretty actress (possessing an attractive play, with a good title and a smart agent) can secure a season or two's successful career, a golden lining to her purse, and a short lived popularity, is too tempting to resist, and outweighs in a measure the early hope and efforts of many talented actresses to build a name "that dies not."

The actresses who play merely for their own pleasure and to gratify their vanity are the offspring of the rage for amateur theatricals that has spread within the last few years throughout the country; and they help to overcrowd our dramatic agencies and provincial theatres. For the applause that greets the amateur actress is divine music, and she must have more of it and is often willing to pay the piper. So, blinded by her own vanity and foolish praise of indulgent friends, she aspires to tread the boards of a real theatre; and, ignorant of the first rules of the stage [and] fortified by a few lessons from some professor of elocution--who, by the way, in nine cases out of ten, will kill whatever spark of natural talent she may possess--becomes too often one of the very many who have "mistaken their vocation." Of this class of actresses we can but say they readily find engagements through money influence, political influence, or the influence combined of pretty faces, pretty figures and exquisite dressing--exquisite dressing being a *desideratum* of the present theatrical age.

Nothing great in acting is expected of them and nothing great in acting is achieved by them. They are admirable, animated fashion plates. And the height of the ambition of an actress of this class is to be called "one of the best dressed women on the stage"; and the lady of fashion who goes to see this butterfly act is questioned on her return home, not "How did she act?" but "What did she wear?" Ill natured people say (But what will not ill natured people say?) that too many of these butterfly actresses usurp the places of their more talented professional sisters, often playing for a merely nominal salary.

But it is of that class of actresses who seriously make acting a business that we must mainly treat. Of the actress who is recognized in the dramatic profession as such, and who applies for an engagement on the strength of being well up in stage business, possessing a good wardrobe and an average amount of talent (in a word, a genuine professional, a real worker in the theatrical beehive), she deserves her apprenticeship, perhaps as a second chambermaid, and rising by degrees to a juvenile lady or first soubrette. If she has a "quick study," she congratulates herself; as well she may, for her profession is then robbed of one of its greatest terrors of her, and her rise is consequently rapid. But if she has a "hard study," her profession is laborious to her indeed, and she "works her way up" slowly. True, her study improves in time; but she is, nevertheless, always afflicted with a certain amount of stage nervousness that no amount of experience can thoroughly divest her of. A long run of a piece she considers a godsend, and trembles at the sight of a part of thirty lengths.

The conscientious, painstaking actress commands our respect and we feel willing to forgive her little harmless vanity, for it is the province of the profession she is in to fan any spark of vanity and self-conceit she may harbor. So who can blame her if, industriously working for a salary, she, too, strives for applause and looks eagerly in the papers to see if they have "noticed her"; for the applause and notice means more to her than mere personal gratification. It whispers of a better position and more salary another season.

Young actresses have their beau ideals of what an actress should be and is, and they sometimes mold themselves consciously, and often unconsciously, on some reigning actress--too often, unfortunately, falling into the model's errors while copying her perfections. In this age, where the tyranny of fashion dictates what women must wear and read and see, it is difficult for the actress to throw off the trammels; for fashion follows her onto the stage, and dictates to her and tells her it is the "stage fashion," and has ever been, to deliver, for instance, the love speech of Pauline to Claude, in "The Lady of Lyons," with unblushing effrontery and with self-possession of a hardened, worldly woman, [rather than] the tender words of a maiden of eighteen. So she must laugh and gesticulate and die on the stage as stage fashion dictates and not as nature teaches. And she obeys, perhaps as long as she lives, perhaps till thought and reflection and golden experience open her eyes and show her at last how to "hold the mirror up to nature." And then the actress too often finds the melancholy truth of the theatrical proverb, "When an actress can act Juliet she no longer looks Juliet," and that is hard. Just when the actress sees what she could do, her looking glass, perhaps relentlessly, says, "Too late."

To those women of the profession, few as we know they are, who are earnestly striving for fame, who spare no exertion or study to improve themselves in their art, we would respectfully say: follow the example of the great French actress, Rachael, and study from nature. When asked to play Adrienne Lecouvreur, [she] said, "It is impossible! I have never seen a woman die of poison! Wait till I have witnessed such a death and I will play the part." Those who saw her enact Adrienne instinctively felt that they were witnessing a copy of nature, and they were right.

[*New York Clipper*, August 3, 1872]

THE ACTRESS' DRESSER

I dress the actresses of the theatre, and my wages is light though my duties are heavy. But "half a loaf's better than none," as I used to say in my younger days, when I was on the stage myself and went on in the ballet and choruses and got four dollars a week. "Far better simple herbs with an honest heart than full and plenty with the stalled ox in sin and assumption," as Shakespeare says. And my meaning is that I'm an honest, upright woman, and folks as knows me from girlhood up can tell you my character and surroundings to a T, or else I'd be ashamed to say, nowadays, I ever went on in the ballet.

But in my younger days ballet girls had clothes on when they went on the stage. Ah, me! Times is changed. And some of them that was in the theatre with me then are fine actresses today. You see, when a woman's got an everlasting hankering on her for acting, she's going to fight her way up somehow; and I suppose if my mind had had a bent that way I might be a star myself, a playing my farewell engagement through the country. But I never had no false ambition, and never had a way of thrusting myself forward when a speaker was wanted to make an announcement. Neither did I ever take it upon myself, if an actress was sick, to declare to the manager that I knew the lines by heart and could go on for the part. Not I. I was always too retiring and kept too much in the background for my own good, a way the ballet at present isn't much troubled with, I can venture. But yet, I got parts, too, and was often selected for my demure and dignified bearing to replace the second old woman. And there wasn't wanting of spiteful, giddy things to say, [like] I was chosen not for my cleverness but because I looked such parts. But I've a mind above the common run, and always imputed such remarks to their ignorance, and as that they didn't know no better.

Neither was I a tittivating myself up and laying myself out to catch a husband; for I'm independent and have got along without one to this day. And I thank my lucky stars, for I've seen the heaps of trouble husbands cause in this business, and I've troubles enough to bear as I am, as the most of dressers have. But the most of them hasn't the advantage that I have had of being once on the stage themselves. For they mostly is merely relatives of someone connected with the stage-- the wardrobe woman's sister, the stage carpenter's wife, and such like-- and haven't got the encyclopedia of theatrical events at their fingers' ends like me, and haven't the power to say to them actresses, who's putting on too many airs altogether in a dressing room to the dresser, as I can:

"Come on, ma'am, you needn't order me round so. I've seen the day when your father was ordered round himself, when he used to carry on chairs and tables at such a theatre years ago."

Or:

"I guess I know what I'm about, for I was in this business before you was born."

Or:

"I suppose you don't remember the time when me and you went on in the ballet together."

And that shuts 'em up on the spot; for you see, when you reckon years up, years will tell you against all the artificial fixings in the world. And that's worse to remind an actress of than that she ever went on in the ballet, for most of 'em are ashamed of that being known. But some of 'em are proud of it, and will say:

"I mounted the tree step by step. I didn't have no influence to put me forward, but had to work my way, through my own talent."

You see I'm a lone woman and have to stand up for myself, and have to take some of the airiest down a peg or there'd be no bearing with 'em. And I think I can do it, for I've got most of the actresses down fine, and the whole pedigree of 'em; indeed, there's but little connected with 'em I don't know. There's a saying, "A hero ain't a hero in his own valley," and I can tell you some of these actresses ain't "divinities" to a dresser's eye. But some of 'em is ladies, and when I'm waiting on a lady I don't think I'm bemeaning myself in so doing; but when I reflect I've been an actress myself, and come to be ordered round by one who calls herself an actress, and don't know no better than not to wear a hoop skirt in a Roman piece, it sets my blood boiling.

I've dressed dozens and dozens of actresses in my time, who, if you'll believe me, didn't know no more how to put their clothes on than a baby; but they was mostly novices. It's all very easy for a novice to get off Lady Teazle, for instance, by heart, and then, with the assistance of an old stager to hammer the stage business into her head, and going over the part for six or eight weeks daily at home, she feels comparatively easy when she comes on stage to rehearse with the real performers; as who wouldn't under the circumstances, with everybody encouraging and smiling and making believe to you you're a doing it beautiful, and nobody to tell you there's someone a giving a little imitation of you in a sly corner when your back's turned. And perhaps she'll carry herself through the performance at night, as to make the public believe she really knows what she's about; for nobody's so easily gulled as the public, as discerning as they think themselves. But wait until the novice comes into my hands to dress, and comes to put on her wig and train, and see how helpless she is. I feel it my duty to tell all such that Rome wasn't built in a day, and if it's true, as old actors say it is--"It takes a man five years to learn to stand still on the stage"--it takes an actress as least as long before she can dress through the range of her drama properly, and know that slippers don't go with a riding habit, nor a lace shawl with a wintry scene, nor earrings in a young officer's disguise ain't proper, and to wear and flirt a train properly isn't achieved by some artists in a lifetime.

And that reminds me, when I see a novice dragging her new white satin train round behind the scene, instead of taking it up over her arm like a woman would who understood her business, I think she's much like the boy with the whistle, and is paying dear for her theatrical experience.

And if there's one thing I abominate more than a novice, it's an actress who is in love; and she's a common nuisance to everybody from the dresser down. In the first place, she neglects her business at rehearsal. She is abstracted, and spends so much time billing and cooing, and driving out, and here and there, that it's ten to one if she looks at the part she's got to play till she gets to the theatre. And she comes flying in to dress at the last moment.

"Oh, Miggs, I'm late," she salutes me with, just as if I couldn't tell her that.

Miggs is a nickname they've given me in the dressing room. I don't mind as long as I get my money. If it amuses them, I have no objection, for trifles amuse little minds. And I can tell you Miggs has her hands full to hustle the young lady's clothes in time to get her on stage at her cue. Why, I'd need to have a dozen hands to manage such a creature. She's nervous and fidgety, and wriggling about, and doing her hair while I'm trying to hook her up. And these actresses do have their clothes made to pinch 'em in to that degree that it makes one's fingers tingle to get them together. I can venture to say that the young lady in question won't be half dressed before she discovers she's left something at home.

"Oh, Miggs, where's my other satin slipper? I thought they were both in my basket."

Or:

"Oh, Miggs, I took my curls home last night to have them done up and forgot to bring them."

Sometimes its the key she's forgot of her dressing case, sometimes her jewels; but whatever it is, I have to post off at all speed back to the hotel or boarding house and fetch the missing article. And when I get back to the theatre, such a tearing and driving to get her ready.

Now I ask anyone how a woman's to get clothes on a lady when she's got a playbook in one hand and a rouge pot in the other, and is reciting one minute and fuming and fretting and scolding and hopping about like a grasshopper.

"Oh, Miggs, I shall never be ready. Oh, good lord, there's the overture. No, no, that waist is for the second . . . 'Who is it that every day . . . who is it that every day sends me these . . .' Oh, heavens, Miggs, there's the coda! Give me some pins. Never mind, I'll fasten it as I go down the stairs. Quick, Miggs, my handkerchief."

And when she gets on the stage, her hurry and agitation have, ten to one, driven what little she did know of her part out of her head. And isn't she blessed by the other performers when she fails to give cues. It's ten to one, too, that she don't have to sidle up to the wing under some pretense and take a property letter or purse or something from the property boy's hands, when she ought to have had them in her pocket before she went on. But she's in love and she don't care. She laughs and thinks it's a fine joke to have kept her diamond rings on in a peasant girl's costume. I can't tell you the times I've been dragged down behind the scenes by some near-sighted, giddy young girl of an actress, just to peep for her into the front of the house to see if a gentleman dressed so and so, with a bouquet in his hands, isn't sitting on the right of the parquet?

"Yes."

And the flutter when he is there. And how the devoted young man is acted to for the rest of the evening. And his Dulcinea, in such a haste to meet him, she steps out of her clothes and into the dressing room with a bound, and goes off with the paint still on her face with her deary to supper.

But commend me to the actress who's got no young man on the brain. She's got manners, she has, and a pleasant word for everybody in the dressing room. And if she's a thorough lady, she makes no rude remarks about anybody; and if any are made in her hearing, she don't pretend to hear 'em. If she's devoted to her profession--and most of actresses, if they ain't to young and skittish, is--why it's probable she'll have no occasion to look at the playbook in the dressing room. She's dead-letter perfect. And she knows what she should wear without me having to tell her. And everything's laid in apple-pie order in her dressing basket. She isn't one of your actresses who hasn't a stitch of wardrobe to their backs, and whose excuse is:

"My trunks are detained in Chicago, or Atlanta, or Salt Lake City, and will be here next week."

I knows what that means. You see it makes me laugh to think these actresses believe they can blind me. I suppose those who put their pads and tights on at home, and come to the theatre in them, think they deceive me. Oh, dear, no! Why none of 'em can do it; nor can they deceive each other, and how hard they try for it. But see when the dressing room door closes on the comedy lady, perhaps descending, dressed for the stage for a new piece, how her dress and appearance and acting and character is all raked over the coals by the other actresses remaining behind. [It's] something astonishing if I wasn't so used to it, and used to the nods and winks and knowing looks and sneering remarks. And if the absent one's dress is very lovely and very costly, her salary is figured up, and the female arithmetician's verdict is:

"The salary couldn't do it!"

But, pshaw! That's only momentary envy and passes off, and perhaps another night the comedy lady will be defended by the very one who assailed her behind her back a few nights before. We all has our faults, and actresses has theirs. But see when one is taken ill, how good them others is to her; and, seeing that, you'd forgive 'em more sins than they really has.

[*New York Clipper*, November 11, 1871]

THE PROMPTER

The model prompter never swears, and his face is always wreathed in smiles. The model prompter is chary in reporting delinquents who keep the stage waiting, and never copies a part for a poor actor and then reminds him that copyists receive so much per length. The model prompter never exacts forfeits, nor reprimands ballet girls for encroaching down the first entrance; indeed, he often surrenders his seat to the prettiest, that she may have a better view of the stage. The model prompter never leaves the book in the call boy's hands while he goes out to see what o'clock it is in a neighboring saloon. The model prompter's grammar may not always be faultless, but his performance on the gong is simply perfection. The model prompter, being only a prompter, and not a diplomatist, bows no lower to the manager's mistress as she passes behind the scenes than to the humblest ballet girl. The model prompter scorns to secure a copy on the sly of any theatrical manuscript entrusted to him, whereby to turn an honest penny. The model prompter would rather starve, indeed, than steal a manuscript. The model prompter, though invariably a temperance man himself, is the last person in the theatre to observe the intoxication of an artist, and never reports such a case if possible. The model prompter is usually a fine actor, but his modesty keeps him in the shade of the prompter's box, from which he only emerges to face the footlights when suddenly called upon to replace some artist who is "indisposed." The model prompter has no time to retail gossip, scandal and small talk; but is always provided with a pocket full of change, ready at any moment to loan a needy actor a little sum.

Seriously though, of all the gay audience assembled within the walls of a metropolitan theatre to witness a night's performance, how many, I wonder, ever deign a thought about the prompter behind the curtain? Just about as many perhaps as there are those among a boat load of excursionists who care to remember there is a pilot at the wheel silently guiding them to their destination. The prompter is generally vaguely recognized by the public as a part and parcel of the mysterious theatrical machinery. And he excites as much universal interest as the proscenium itself does, by which he stands. The uninitiated, when remembering the existence of the prompter at all, have a misty mental vision of a man comfortably seated in a cozy armchair, indolently holding a book of the play, and, before the rise of the curtain, lazily stretching forth his hand to give the curtain bell a jerk, and then yawning the remainder of the evening over his book, occasionally throwing the word to some actor or actress not quite *au fait* in their respective parts; meanwhile, blowing a silver whistle from time to time to change the scenes.

But the initiated know the prompter as he really exists, know the responsibility of his thankless position, and the weary and laborious life he leads. They know when the rehearsal is over, and every member of the company is at liberty to go where they will, the prompter, too often, must remain behind to make out his scene plot, his property plot, etc., and to write any letters that may be required on the stage in the coming evenings performance; perhaps to copy a part or two as well, and a dozen other duties of his calling too tedious to mention here. The initiated know that he is saddled with many disagreeable duties not set down in his engagement and properly belonging to the management: perhaps to notify an actor that his services will be dispensed with after such a date, to hint to an actress her dress does not please the taste of the manager, or to suggest to a singer the omission of a song, as it doesn't "go."

The prompter is the one man of the company who never has a night off. He could never say last winter, "I'm finished in the second act, and I'll drop into Niblo's in time for the 'Naucht girl's dance'"; nor this summer, "I am through in the third scene, and I'll see the last act of *Elfie* at Wallack's." No, be the play what it may, the prompter must be at his post till the curtain rises and falls upon it. There is no holiday for him while the season lasts; and the theatre to the prompter, like the mangle to Mr. Mantalini, is "one infernal dem'd grind."

The debut of a novice is a trying ordeal to the prompter as well as the debutante. He watches the new hero or heroine with an anxious brow, he is at the wing where he or she makes the first entrance, and he is at another wing at the exit to show the bewildered novice the next place of entrance. And the prompter follows line by line every word uttered by the new beginner. What a pity the trembling novice cannot catch the few brief words of criticism that the prompter whispers in a friend's ear at his elbow, for his is an opinion "as is an opinion." And from his silent corner, through many successive seasons, he has witnessed many a scene not set down in the play.

On the first night of a new season, as each new artist makes his or her entrance and exit, the prompter mentally checks each one off.

"Ah, you'll do. You understand your business."

"My friend, you're not the style for this shop; that kind of acting won't go down here."

"Ah, you're full of gig, a stunner."

"You played in London at the Haymarket, did you? Well, I wonder they could bear to part with you. You can go back there, for you'll get your walking papers here in about two weeks."

"That woman's only fit for the ballet. How the dickens did she ever get the position here?"

It does not take the prompter long to learn the peculiarities of the members of the company. He soon knows that man who "flutes" through every part, and is always in need of his assistance. He soon discovers that Mr. Blank never studies much else but cues, and Mr. Somebody-else who never gives a cue, and that pest of an actor whom it is impossible to follow in the prompt book. The prompter is a silent witness of many humors, tempers and strange passions. He should be a good judge of human nature, for he has excellent opportunity to study it, not on the stage, but behind the scenes, a little world of itself, where bloodless battles are fought, petty malice shown, where the tattler thrives, and the "school for scandal" is played every night of the season.

The first night of a new piece is one of some anxiety to the prompter; and the first night of a show piece is a night of agony and suspense to him: the orchestra to ring in, calls for the company, the curtain to ring up and down on every act, warning bells for traps, for sky borders, for trick changes, for scenes, for gaslights, for gauzes; and the dialogue on the stage to follow meanwhile, bewildered supernumeraries to hustle on the stage and frantically beckon off, giddy ballet girls to silence and to keep from rushing on at any moment, and to send on at the right [time], dozens of chattering enquirers to answer, and dozens of remarks from all sorts of people to listen to.

"What scene do we go on in?"

"Where do I get my spear?"

"Do I come on from the right or the left?"

"Can you tell me where my sister dresses?"

"Oh, for God's sake, I've lost my part! Let me look at the book."

"I come up a trap. How do I get under the stage?"

"Is it me now?"

"They can't find the page's dress for me!"

"Is it me now?"

"My dancing partner, Miss Smith, is in a faint down in the dressing room. What am I to do?"

"Is it me now?"

"Say, they'll have to keep up that front scene; we can't set the grotto in time."

"For heaven's sake, when that man comes off tell him he mustn't rant like that."

"Lower those borders."

"Can you tell me if this is my helmet?"

"The table shouldn't be on that side the stage."

"We rehearsed it that way this morning, sir."

"I tell you we didn't."

"I tell you we did."

"Say, they can't work that trick chair."

"What the devil do you let those women make that noise for?"

"Good Lord, look here, this isn't the kind of dagger I should have."

"Don't change yet, the scene ain't ready."

"There's no stepladder for me to get up to that balcony."

"Look out for those guns, now."

"Monsieur, where is it den I get de rosin for my shoes?"

"Look out for those guns!"

"See here, they've got a wood wing on in that palace scene."

"What shall I do? I came from the other side and I can't get across the stage now?"

"Damn it all, I ought to have two pistols!"

"I can't open the door. Which way does it open?"

"That woman did not give me a single cue!"

"Look out for those calcium lights!"

And the prompter's culminating agony is a transformation scene: agitated ballet women to get in their places, agitated carpenters to direct, agitated gas men to shout to, agitated property men to yell after, and an agitated audience stomping and calling impatiently to add to the excitement. But the curtain is rung down at last and the exhausted prompter gladly leaves the hot theatre, choking with sulfur and gun powder and gas and burning rosin, and happily breaths the purer atmosphere without once more.

But the piece is a success; at least the public say so, who come pouring out of the theatre, profuse in praise and admiration of everything and everybody. Even the despised supers are remembered; and it is remarked how well trained they were and what an excellent appearance they made, and the dancers and the scenery. Nothing is forgotten except the prompter. Nobody thinks of him, nobody says he carried the piece through with scarcely a hitch--and the first night, too, and so much upon his hands. And the critics next morning compliment everybody, even to the carpenters; but they never give the prompter a line. Yes, the piece is a success and there is no doubt it will have a long run. Just think of a man undergoing this prompter's experience of this night (a little mitigated, it's true) for one or two hundred consecutive nights! Truly, the prompter "is worthy of his hire."

[*New York Clipper*, February 24, 1872]

THE CALL BOY

His age in his noviciate ranges from twelve to fourteen. He is, indeed, the smallest twig we find shooting forth on the theatrical tree. And his child existence is of a theatrical hot house growth; for his dramatic schooling is with, as a rule, superlatively worldly men and superlatively worldly women. And early fed on all the good and all the evil springing from that peculiar tree, the tree of theatrical knowledge, he seldom fails in one or two brief seasons to bloom forth a knowing blade, with "an old head on young shoulders," a cute customer indeed-- in a word, a genuine call boy of the period.

And now he has reached his sixteenth year; and, if so, he has certainly achieved his first ambition and carries a watch, perhaps 'tis only silver, attached with a natty ribbon to his buttonhole. But as to his time, he will vouch for its correctness to a second against any gold chronometer in the theatre; and at the commencement and close of each performance, compares it with the green room clock with the profoundest gravity. And to all his duties that pertain to his calling, [he] is as systematic as the director of a bank.

Promptly at his post beside the prompter's desk at night, and at the prompter's table in the morning, to the minute, he pins his faith on the prompter and stands a little in awe of him. He is a little shy of the stage

manager, too, always provided the stage manager understands his business; for if there be the slightest flaw in that gentleman's managerial tactics, the call boy's quick eye detects it. And who has such opportunities for so doing as he? In such a case, the secret contempt he feels is unbounded.

The call boy rarely aspires to become an actor; and when he does, he is an exceptional case. When he does go on for a part, everybody behind the scenes evinces a more than common interest in him; and there's not an actor in the place who would think of refusing him the loan of any article of dress for the occasion, from the page's scarf to the plumes in his hat, for he is a general favorite. His own views as to the merits of the acting he sees may not be strictly reliable, and it is to be feared that the star who has been most munificent in remembering the call boy the last night of the engagement will always rank highest in his eyes as an artist. But his ambition pointing oftener toward the prompter's desk than to the footlights, his brain is ever busy with the hope of one day reigning there himself; and when that day comes, as it surely will--for he is in excellent training for the post--what a prompter he will make!

He sails smoothly now, meanwhile, towards his goal. But he has had his skirmishes in previous seasons; [and] in those skirmishes has learned the rocks and shoals of theatrical waters, and has found a way to steer adroitly clear of most of them. No female blandishments can now seduce him into becoming the champion in a ballet girl's green room or dressing room quarrel. By no slip of the tongue will he now repeat to the soubrette what he overheard the low comedian say about her being a "muff," and the impossibility of "working a scene with her." No bribe can now tempt him to smuggle in a glass of brandy to that ever thirsty individual, when against the rules of the theatre. And no cajoling can induce him to reveal the name of the piece, if still withheld from publicity, that is in preparation at the theatre where he is employed. All these errors are as things of the past for which he has suffered. He has had his lesson and will profit by it.

But let him steer his course as cautiously as he may, there are often breakers ahead that he sees but feels he cannot overcome. Let him make his calls ever so punctually from the green room, there is always someone, when late for the stage, to put the blame on him and swear "he never was called." Let the call boy hasten with all dispatch to fasten up the "10 o'clock sharp" call for the morrow's rehearsal long before any of the performers have left the theatre for the night, and perhaps he will be told point blank by some actress tomorrow morning, when she comes hurrying onto the stage at eleven, that "the call wasn't up when she left the theatre," and the call boy will be reprimanded by the management for his negligence. And what does the call boy say? He says but little; he has done his duty, and leaves the manager to find out as he may the petty shifts that negligent people resort to in the profession. And what does he think? He thinks if Hotspur had been attending to his business, instead of telling his fellow actors what a hit he made in that very part at such a theatre with Mr. Phelps or Mr. Buchanan or Mr. Kean or Mr. Somebody-else, why he would have heard the call, that's all. And if Parthenia went home at night as soon as the performance was over, instead of going to an oyster supper and sitting up till two in the morning, why maybe then she'd manage to get up in time for a ten o'clock rehearsal.

Indeed, most of the call boy's annoyances arise from the negligence of others. He is reprimanded again and again for not calling in the parts of such a piece when the run of the piece is over, and he has asked and asked the artists individually for them until he is weary.

"I'll bring my part tomorrow."

"You shall have the part tonight."

And that's all that comes of it. But he is persevering, is the call boy, and will dog at this actor or that actress till they are fain to remember the parts to get rid of his importunity.

But he has duties not so irksome. He likes to carry the copy of the house bills and posters to the printing office, and the advertisements to the newspapers. He seems to know everybody and everybody him, though only by his surname (and few in the theatre know him by any other). He picks up bits of information in this office and catches a few words of an interesting conversation in that [one]; and, while waiting about in another, scrapes acquaintance with a printer's devil downstairs and asks a few questions about his trade. He is often sent to the houses of different actors and actresses by the prompter, with the calls--in cases where performers, absent from the previous night's performance, are not cognizant of the coming rehearsal--and sees these gods and goddesses of the drama in their home *dishabillé*.

The call boy is seldom present during an entire rehearsal, being dispatched here and there--to the post office, to a theatrical bookstore, to another theatre to see if Mr. Such-a-One can be spared to perform such a part in the case of some sudden dilemma, dispatched to see what detains the star, or sent to hunt up that unfortunate actor who never attends a rehearsal in proper time and knows but little about his part when he does arrive. [Such an actor] is quite unreliable by night as well as by day; but somehow he's always in an engagement and gets but little reprimanded by the manager and but little fault found with him by the actors and actresses whom he detains and too often embarrasses. He will be recognized by all professional people as one of those famed children of his profession, as one who seems to have "his honors thrust upon him."

The call boy is *au fait* with regard to all the stores in town where theatrical goods are to be purchased. And to whom does the new French dancer apply for information relative to dancing shoes? To those of her own sex in the theatre? No, but to the call boy. And he'll warn her of the place where snide dancing shoes, with no stiffening in the toes, are sold, and which wouldn't last her the night through; and warns other prospective buyers from suspicious tarnished spangle dealers and suspicious "good night colored satins." Goodness knows where he gets his information, but he is generally [a] reliable authority. By ten o'clock at night he'll tell you "that new piece up at such a theatre, or down at such a theatre, is a fizzle, or hit 'em heavy," as the case may be. He's heard the news before anyone about him behind the scenes, whilst shooting in and out at the stage door.

The call boy has an eye to speculation, and often turns an honest penny by introducing second-hand stage dresses, brought by needy folks to the back door, [for which he] gets a little percentage for his troubles. But in whatever transaction employed (save when making love), he always bears himself with a certain stateliness. Like the barber in Nicholas Nickleby, he finds it essential to his dignity to "draw a line somewhere"; and he stops at a super, though he will accept a few cigars from the hands of that individual, who is perchance employed in a tobacco manufactory in the daytime. But he receives them as a testimonial to his position as call boy at the theatre.

The call boy is susceptible to the tender passion, and falls in love many times during a season. And if he be particularly engaging, [he] is the object of considerable rivalry on the part of the ballet girls, the prettiest among whom he generally sees some after the performance. But, in truth, he is somewhat of a male flirt, and will cut a ballet girl to accompany some pretty actress home. But, if she be old and ugly, he must allow himself to be often victimized, and is fertile with excuses, his standing one being, "he'd be very happy, but he has to go right away to the telegraph office for the manager."

When the ballet girls have secretly determined on playing an innocent ruse on some vain coxcomb of the theatre, who fancies every girl who looks at him is in love with him, who is chosen to carry out the ruse but the call boy. And how gravely he presents the note and bouquet to the gull, carelessly remarking, "Left at the stage door for you." And how patiently he waits the next day at some appointed place out of sight, with a knot of giggling ballet ladies, to watch the dupe advance in expectation of meeting the fair unknown writer of the *billet*.

But the night's performance is about to commence, and he makes his music calls and his calls for the first act. And now we find him, perhaps, under the stage in the music room, picking up scraps of French and German, and listening to the history of Herr Schmidt's violin, a real Amati. And here he is again, waiting by a trap under the stage, [for] it's his duty to stop the three fairies [from] giggling and "ohing," and [from] their little shrieks of alarm as they go jerking up to public view. And here's the call boy, now waiting at the door of some actress' dressing room, and calling to her [that] she has only two minutes more for her change. And now he's in the green room shouting his calls for the next act; and the next instant, way up in the wardrobe, sent by the manager to know why in the world Mr. So-and-So's dress isn't ready and down in the dressing room. And now, being near the paint room, he flies in there to see how they're getting on with the scenes for the new show piece that they're obliged to work on, now by night as well as day, to be ready in time. And the scene painter's even glad to see him (who is proverbial for being glad to see no one in his paint room). And see, the call boy's actually helping them to put the fire on the palace scene. Nothing seems to come amiss to him. And now he's down behind the scenes again, listening to something the stage carpenters are saying.

And so he goes on from day to day and night to night, getting valuable knowledge, for the vision haunts his dreams of being one day not only a prompter but a manager; and should his dreams ever come true, what a host of useful information he will have in store to fitly fill the position. How soon his keen eye will detect the substitute in his orchestra, too many feet of lumber in the stage carpenter's bill for any theatrical bridge, the frauds of the wardrobe, the frauds of the property room; how well he will be prepared to meet them all. Meanwhile, he sails along, his trim figure neatly attired, with a little display of cheap jewelry and a little conceit, but a close business lad, a genuine call boy of the period.

[*New York Clipper*, December 2, 1871]

THE STAGE DOORKEEPER
by Bambrino

I'm the stage doorkeeper of the theatre. I've tended stage door the best part of seven years; and therefore I ought to be privileged, I think, to know and to be able to say something about it. I don't know that I should ever have thought of doing so but for a remark an English swell actor made the other night.

"Billy," says he, "Dickens says, 'The stage door has quite a shame-faced look, as if conscious of being unlike any other door.'"

Now, do you know that remark hurt me? Not but what it might be just enough, for I know our stage door is rather shabby looking, not having seen a coat of paint in many a year, and having no bell or knocker, [it] does look unlike ordinary doors. But when a man's been sitting the best part of seven years in one place, he gets kind of attached to it and don't care to hear remarks made about it, at least by anybody but himself. And with thinking how long I had sat there, and the world of people I'd seen pass in and out by that same doorway, and one little circumstance and another coming up to my mind, it fell out I wrote down (having plenty of time on my hands) my experience at the stage door, and this is it:

It has taught me that no matter how humble a man's position may be he can't learn how to fill it, to say properly, in a day's time. Why I was a whole season before I knew how to tend the stage door as it ought to be tended. First, because I used to get restive, sitting so long in one place, so many hours at a time. And when I tired reading the newspaper, I felt a strong inclination to stretch my legs for a block or two; but that's against orders, and I found I had to curb that. Again, the curiosity would be strong on me at times to see what was going on inside the stage, for the music and the voices would tempt me to steal down the passageway and look at a rehearsal or performance. That's against orders, too. But the desire gradually wore off, and it came to be an old story to me; and now I care nothing to see a rehearsal, and seldom to see a performance.

Sometime of a week night, and when I know everybody who has any business in the building is inside it, and it's past the hour for any of my usual callers--for I have my regular callers every day and night--I do saunter in occasionally, perhaps down as far as the third or fourth entrance, and take a look at what's going on on the stage. But when I've looked at the dresses and the scene and the general appointments, I'm satisfied, for listening to the play would be about as interesting as opening a strange book haphazard and reading an odd chapter.

It took me some time, too, to learn who had a right to be admitted to the stage door and who hadn't. And they once had a rare laugh at me for stopping the new stage manager, but how was I to know him till I'd had him identified to me? So many people had played their tricks upon me so often, persuading me to let them pass in who had no business to be let in at all, that it nearly cost me my situation, and it taught me to keep my weather eye a little wider open. But I'll defy anybody to hocus me nowadays with, "I have a particular appointment with the stage manager," or "I'm an intimate friend of Mr. Leading Man." Oh, no! I find it still hard, however, to deny the ladies, who wish "to see the manager," admittance when he don't want to see them. But I'm a deal more proof than I once was against the influence of fine clothes and a lovely complexion. But, after all, they're more difficult to get rid of than the men; and I've found that generally the manager himself is far more in dread of being pestered by them, for he can dismiss a man easily enough, but a woman will always have the last word.

You may ask what do all these strangers who are not engaged in the theatre want there? Why, some of them to get engagements; if not for themselves, for their sisters or brothers or wives or children. Heaven preserve me, what a world of clever children there are (in the dramatic way), that is, if you'd believe all their parents say of 'em. For a great many people actually tell me the errand they've come upon, just as if I, the stage doorkeeper, had a spark of influence or could help them one jot. A great many try the front of the house, at the box office first; and, getting no satisfaction, they come to the stage door to try their luck here. I envy the treasurer that little window of his; for when people bore him too long, all he's got to do is lower that little slide and shut them out, and that settles it. But I have no such defense; and you wouldn't credit me how I'm harassed with one and another, not to mention the incessant repetition of the questions by men connected with our stage, "Billy, have you got any tobacco?"

And experience has taught me to say, "No." And, really, I haven't been known to have any tobacco for many a day. Not to mention, either, the ragged urchins who, from hour to hour, are ducking their heads inquisitively in at the stage door, burning with desire to penetrate the mystery of behind the scenes. And it's a relief to me when I know the hour is past to expect many more of them, [and so] to have a quiet chat with the policeman on his beat in our neighborhood about the affairs of the nation.

Ah, but the poor actors who are hard up, have been out of engagements some time (I almost know from their appearance.), and who look so anxious and so care worn, and inquire so eagerly for the manager, that I do feel glad if an interview's granted them, even if they shouldn't succeed in getting engaged, for at least it puts 'em out of their suspense, and that's an awful thing, is suspense. I've seen so many theatrical people suffering from it. For instance, an actor, new to the theatre perhaps, [and] new to the town, [is] in suspense whether he'll hit the public. Ah, I can see it written on his face as he comes through the stage door at night to dress. God knows, perhaps [there is] a wife and family depending on the chances of his success of that night; and if he does make a hit, how lively he comes down the stairs when the ordeal is over, and how cheerily he says to me, "Good night."

I can generally tell who has made a hit and whether the piece is a success without anyone saying a word to me on the subject. Yes, and I can tell by the same token if the house is good or poor. How? By the applause. You see, I'm something in the position of a blind man. I can't see what's going on inside there, but I can hear; and experience and long habit has taught me to notice the sounds I hear, more acutely perhaps than those who are looking on. And when I hear the applause come in a kind of stifled way, no matter how loud, and a humming sound with it as well, I know then the house is packed to suffocation. And when it comes clear and ringing, I'm pretty sure there's plenty of empty seats.

I've learned, too, to distinguish the different kinds of applause. There's the applause of [the] reception of a stranger. It's purely mechanical in a double sense, and very different from the sound that greets

an old friend. Enthusiastic applause, tolerant applause, reluctant applause, I know 'em all. And I know, when a piece has run a few nights, about the time to expect the volley of musketry, the shriek of the female in distress, the chorus, etc., and that one tearing, stamping round of applause, accompanied by a yell and a few shrill whistles, and then I know the comedian has said something, the like of which, when I was a young man and sat looking at a play with my sweetheart beside me, made me wish she wasn't there.

But I'm wandering away again from my customers, as I call them. There are many of them who don't come seeking engagements, but come to exhibit a new invention or some improvement in working stage machinery, or the lights, or the scenes, or something in that way. Sometimes it's a newly patented improved chair for the parquet, sometimes a wonderful ventilator, or a machine to cool the theatre in the summer time, and a hundred things we are bored with and that I'll consequently not annoy you with.

Some come for the address of a certain actor, oftener for the address of a certain actress. Many have subscription lists. Others want the theatre for a charitable benefit for some institution. And a few come dunning the poor players who are in arrears. But I think that's taking a mean advantage of a man, to come blurting out, before everybody hanging about the stage door, that Mr. So-and-So owes two week's board and won't pay it, or such a one owes a washing bill and won't be prompt; a mean advantage and I never countenance it. Some seedy stragglers wait about the stage door until the rehearsal is over to tackle an unsuspecting friend as he comes out, hoping he'll stand treat. And prosperous actors are on the alert then to narrate their late brilliant successes in Pen Yan.

But of all my customers, heaven spare me from the would be dramatic authors. They seldom come to the stage door, but bother the people in the front of the house; and where I see one author, they see twenty, [which] the treasurer once assured me when I was telling him what a nuisance they were. But some of them will leave their manuscripts in my care for the manager. And they're conceited enough to put the price sometimes on the back of them, just as if they were sure they were going to be bought off hand. And then they begin, day after day, "Has a note or manuscript been left in your charge for me?"
And it almost invariably turns out that the manuscript is left for them, and always accompanied with a note. I can't forget one man. He'd been

coming to the stage door every day for two weeks. Somehow his manuscript got mislaid, and he swore at last that he'd sue the management for its value. But finally it turned up, I suppose, for it was put in my hands to be returned to its owner, which, when he called again, I did accordingly. He took it sulkily enough and went his way. But in a few moments he comes flying back.

"See here," he says, "this manuscript has never been read."

"Hasn't it, sir," says I.

"No. I can take my oath of it."

"Perhaps, sir," says I in a kind of conciliating way, "perhaps, sir, it didn't suit."

"How could they tell whether it would suit or not when they never read it?" he asks indignantly. "Look here," he adds, "and here. Do you see? I pasted the edges of these leaves together myself, and they've never been opened; consequently, the drama has never been read. And I tell you, this treatment is an imposition on dramatic authors, a willful deprivation of the public, a burning, disgraceful imposition!" And he disappeared, raving like a maniac.

But I have daintier things than manuscripts often left in my charge, charming little nosegays and delicate little scented notes. And it's some pleasure to deliver them.

Then there are a different class of callers at the stage door. And they're there at night, mysterious people who prowl about, hanging round the stage door two and three hours at a stretch, who never make any inquiries of me, and have nothing to say to me. They're a different class again from the well dressed young fools who stand round to watch the younger and prettier actresses go in and out at the stage door. No, these strange beings ain't impelled by any curiosity that I can see. They ain't waiting for anybody or anything in particular. And bye and bye they'll flit away as mysteriously as they came. I've been here a long time, as I've told you, but I never could make out what they want.

Then there are some of those who come to accompany the actresses home at night after the performance is over. Sometimes younger brothers, as impertinent and rude imps as one might see. They whistle, they stamp about, and are as restless as beasts in a cage, muttering and growling.

"I wonder if she's ever coming! I wonder if she thinks I've got nothing else to do but stand round here all night! Oh, there you are! You're a pretty one, ain't you, to keep a fellow waiting! Confound you, does it take you two hours to get your street clothes on? Why, you're the last one! I tell you, you are, you slow poke! Raining? Of course it's raining. Umbrella? No, I brought no umbrella. You ain't sugar, are you? You won't melt, will you? Come on, now."

But the young lover, who waits at the stage door for his sweetheart, catch him getting impatient or uttering a murmur. Bless you, he'd wait till morning for her, if need be. Catch him coming without an umbrella if it rains, or a carriage even, if he can afford it.

"I'm afraid I kept you waiting, my dear."

"Oh no, Mary, don't mention it, darling."

And away they go, arm in arm, as loving as two turtle doves, a pretty picture. Ah me! But I've lived to often see the reverse of that picture.

But who's this poorly attired woman who stands waiting silently and patiently at the stage door, and who looks so anxiously every time a step is heard coming down the stairs? An actor's wife. And she's come to try and induce him to go home, instead of wending his way (as is his usual custom) to a drinking saloon hard by. Sometimes she succeeds, but oftener she does not, and goes away with a sigh, sadly, by herself.

And who's this young lady who came down the stairs full an hour ago and is still waiting here at the stage door when everybody else has gone, and who looks tired and a little haggard? Why, this is Mary. She's married now, and here comes her husband to fetch her at last, and not walking as steadily as I could wish to see.

"Oh, George, how long you've kept me waiting."

"You be blowed. Where's that bouquet?"

"What bouquet?"

"Oh, you know. I was in front and I saw the ass that flung it."

"I gave it away."

"You lie! I know you, I know your tricks, and I tell you . . ."

"Hush, George. Come, dear, you've been drinking a little and don't know what you're saying. Come."

They're gone! And here's the watchman to take my place, a welcome relief. And I wish my readers a kind goodnight as the stage door closes on me and my experience.

[*New York Clipper*, December 23, 1871]

PART II: BEHIND THE FOOTLIGHTS

THE "REALISTIC" ON THE STAGE

"Realistic" is a pet word of the day, and with none more so than with those whose province it is to make out the programs and advertisements for our theatres. The word meets us in every variety of color and type on bills and posters. Of the so-called "realistic effects" in our theatres, we have many, and most of them are very charming. The gurgling rivulet of real water in *School*, the past dramatic season; the effective rainstorm of real water in *Lost*, produced some years ago; and the many fountains that of late have gushed with real water so refreshingly in comedy and drama; are all vast improvements on the old "set waters" of gauze or layers of plate glass, or the rattling of shot supposed to be rain, or the twisting round and round in a canvas fountain of that hideous column that we were to imagine water, but that looked indeed like a huge stick of lemon candy endowed with motion.

Today our stage drawing rooms and boudoirs and salons are set with real rosewood furniture, mirrors, lace curtains, tapestry, chandeliers, billiard tables, grand pianos, ormolu clocks and ornaments. In melodrama and tragedy we have knights in real armor, a corps of real drummers, real Arabs, real Indians, and almost real lightning and thunder. In our comedies the actresses wear real diamonds, real laces, real silks and satins, and of the best and of the fashion of real women of fashion. In pantomimes, spectacles, and sensational dramas of the day we have real horses, real donkeys, real dogs, and in "Griffith Gaunt" we had even a real pig. Great Heaven! What can we desire? Perhaps a little more real acting, for instance.

The "realistic effects," such as we are treated to and receive with a round of applause and think no more about afterwards, were but vaguely dreamt or thought of fifteen or twenty years ago, whether by scene painters, stage carpenters or machinists, or by gas or property men. Let any old playgoer recall the inevitable garden set in "The

Hunchback," "Love's Sacrifice," "London Assurance," and dozens of other plays: the faded, patched green baize that covered the stage, but never the visible entrances; the two dusky, dusty, finger-smeared profile marble-painted urns right and left of the fourth entrance, blooming therein the brick dust, exaggerated cabbage roses and impossible blue-green foliage; with a flat in the back sadly at variance with what is to-day the recognized law of perspective--dim, vague, an Athenian temple, a dingy sky that almost touched a wilderness beyond of harassing brown, ultramarine blue, and startling green trees.

Visit any well appointed theatre tonight and, should there be a garden set, mark the vast change and improvement in the minutest detail. The hideous sky borders have vanished and given place to beauteous interlacing vines, or beauteous and faithful copies of fleecy clouds. We have garden paths, a greensward, real flowers, real statues, the dying or brilliant sunlight, delicious moonlight that either floods or fades from the scene at the wave of a magician, the lovely landscape in the distance, the rustic garden chairs on which recline elegantly dressed women.

Turning from the stage, note the improvements everywhere manifest, tending to the comforts of the audience; and the spectator must frankly confess that the architect, scene painter, stage carpenter, machinist, and indeed all, down to the most humble mechanic, have in the last twenty years made rapid strides in their several departments.

But the spectator must need sigh in regret that he cannot compliment the players with a like advancement in their line of business, especially if he has been present any night the past season during the run of a certain play produced in most "realistic" style at Booth's Theatre, where more than one half the people on the stage could not even correctly pronounce the name of the play they were acting in. A few called it "The Woman of Fire," many "The Woman of Iron," etc. In an age in which at least a smattering of French is so easily gained by the dullest individual of an ordinary education, for actors and actresses on the stage of a metropolitan theatre to betray so woefully, as in the above mentioned case, their utter ignorance of what is undoubtedly an essential in the dramas now in vogue, merits at least this allusion to the fact.

And let actors and actresses remember that, the more "realistic" the stage effects, the want of "realistic" in their acting becomes more glaring by comparison. Acting is an art--possibly the most difficult art in the world--and Mr. Edwin Forrest's advice to those who acted with him was, "Never speak a line on the stage the meaning of which you do not fully understand." The author of "Fugitives from Labor" tells us, "All power of illustration implies a habit of vigilant observation." And if we are to ever have truly "realistic" acting, this habit of vigilant observation must become more general than it is today among our players. One might think the above quoted author had certain members of the theatre in his mind's eye where he says, "What is the minimum of work on which a clever creature like myself can live?"

But all honor where honor is due. We have many, hard working students in the dramatic profession; and one of the most earnest is Miss Clara Morris, from whom we are to expect some rare "realistic" acting in the play of The Sphinx, since she crosses the briny deep, it is said, to study the effective acting of the dying scene of a French actress. This is a very good move. But if Miss Morris had only followed the great Rachel's example and studied her poisoning scene (as Rachel did hers) in the hospital, that would have been superlatively "realistic," and would have been a splendid advertisement for the theatre where the play is to be produced. But to study from nature has not become fashionable among our artists.

> Thus nature dwells within our reach;
> But though we stand so near her,
> We still interpret half her speech
> With ears too dull to hear her.

Many years ago the writer witnessed a performance of *Romeo and Juliet* at the Walnut Street Theatre, Philadelphia. Miss Eliza Logan played Juliet, Mrs. Lizzie Weston Davenport (the present Mrs. Charles Mathews) personated Romeo, and a young gentleman named Howard (a very good actor) was Tybalt. In the third act at the cue, "There comes the furious Tybalt back again," Tybalt entered, and he was soon engaged in combat with Romeo. Romeo stabbed him and Tybalt fell, but fell unlike any Tybalt we had ever seen before or have seen since; for any action more singular or clumsy we never witnessed on the stage. The audience tittered, utterly ignorant that they had just seen a most "realistic" effect, and one not set down in the bills. For to the dismay of the Romeo of the night, it was soon discovered that he had really stabbed Tybalt, though, fortunately, not very seriously; but seriously enough to make Mr. Howard forget the fall in the traditional stage way, and causing him, in his agony, to fall instead, as nature dictated.

Mr. Dickens in "Nicholas Nickleby" alludes to a stage "realistic" effect as follows: "We had a first-tragedy man in our company once, who, when he played Othello, used to black himself all over. But that's feeling a part and going into it as if you meant it; it isn't usual, more's the pity."

[*New York Clipper*, July 4, 1874]

STAGE BANQUETS

A veteran actor of inferior fame once expressed his extreme dislike to what he was pleased to term "the sham wine parties" of Macbeth and others. He was weary of the Barmecide banquets of the stage, of affecting to quaff with gusto imaginary wine out of empty pasteboard goblets; and of making believe to have an appetite for wooden apples and "property" comestibles. He was in every sense a poor player, and had often been a very hungry one. He took especial pleasure in remembering the entertainments of the theatre in which the necessities of performance, or regard for rooted tradition, involved the setting of real edible food before the actors. At the same time he greatly lamented the limited number of dramas in which these precious opportunities occurred.

He had grateful memories of the obsolete Scottish melodrama of "Cramond Brig"; for in this work, old custom demanded the introduction of a real sheep's head with accompanying "trotters." He told of a northern British manager who was wont--especially when the salaries he was supposed to pay were somewhat in arrears and he desired to keep his company in good humor and, maybe, alive--to produce this play on Saturday nights. For some days before the performance the dainties that were destined to grace it underwent exhibition in the green-room. A label bore the inscription:

"This sheep's head will appear in the play of "Cramond Brig" on next Saturday night. God save the King."

"It afforded us two famous dinners," reveals the veteran. "We had a large pot of broth made with the head and feet. These we ate on Saturday night. The broth we had on Sunday."

So in another Scottish play, The Gentle Shepherd, of Allan Ramsay, it was long a custom on stages north of the Tweed to present a real haggis, although niggardly managers were often tempted to substitute for the genuine dish a far less savory, if more wholesome, mess of oatmeal. But a play more famous still for the reality of its victuals, and better known to modern times, was Prince Hoare's musical farce, "No Song, No Supper." A steaming hot, boiled leg of lamb and turnips may be described as quite the leading character in the entertainment. Without this appetizing addition, the play has never been represented. There is a story, however, which one can only hope is correct, of an impresario of Oriental origin who supplied the necessary meal; yet, subsequently, fined his company all round on the ground that they had "combined to destroy certain properties of the theatre."

There are many other plays in the course of which genuine food is consumed on the stage. But some excuse for the generally fictitious nature of theatrical repasts is to be found in the fact that eating during performance is often a very difficult matter for the actors to accomplish. Michael Kelly, in his memoirs, relates that he was required to eat part of a fowl in the supper scene of a bygone operatic play called "A House to be Sold." Bannister at rehearsal had informed him that it was very difficult to swallow food on the stage. Kelly was incredulous, however.

"But strange as it may appear," he writes, "I found it a fact that I could not get down a morsel. My embarrassment was a great source of fun to Bannister and Suett, who were both gifted with the accommodating talent of stage feeding. Whoever saw poor Suett as the lawyer in "No Song, No Supper," tucking in his boiled leg of lamb, or in "The Siege of Belgrade," will be little disposed to question my testimony to the fact."

From this account, however, it is manifest that the difficulty of "stage feeding," as Kelly calls it, is not invariably felt by all actors alike. And probably, although the appetites of the superior players may often fail them, the supernumerary or the representative of minor characters could generally contrive to make a respectable meal if the circumstances of the case supplied the opportunity.

The difficulty that attends eating on the stage does not, it would seem, extend to drinking; and sometimes the introduction of real and potent liquors during the performance has led to unfortunate results. Thus, Wincop, who, in 1747, published a tragedy called

"Scanderberg", adding to it "A List of All the Dramatic Authors, with Some Accounts of Their Lives, etc.," describes a curious occurrence at the Theatre Royal in 1693. A comedy entitled "The Wary Widow; or, Sir Noisy Parrot," written by one Higden and now a very scarce book, had been produced. But on the first representation "the author had contrived so much drinking of punch in the play that the actors almost all got drunk, and were unable to get through with it; so that the audience was dismissed at the end of the third act." Upon subsequent performances of the comedy, no doubt the manager reduced the strength of the punch, or substituted some harmless beverage, toast and water perhaps, imitative of that ardent compound so far as mere color was concerned.

There have been actors, however, who have refused to accept the inane semblance of vinous liquor supplied by the management, and especially when, as part of their performance, they were required to simulate intoxication. A certain representative of Cassio was wont to take to the theatre a bottle of claret from his own cellar, whenever he was called upon to sustain that character. It took possession of him too thoroughly, he said with a plausible air, to allow of his affecting inebriety after holding an empty goblet to his lips, or swallowing mere toast and water or small beer. Still his precaution had its disadvantages. The real claret he consumed might make his intemperance somewhat too genuine and accurate, and his portrayal of Cassio's speedy return to sobriety might be in such wise very difficult of accomplishment.

So there have been players of dainty taste, who, required to eat in the presence of the audience, have elected to bring their own provisions, from some suspicion of the quality of the food provided by the management. We have heard of a clown who, entering the theatre nightly to undertake the duties of his part, was observed to carry with him always a neat, paper parcel.

"What did it contain?" bystanders inquired of each other.

Well, in the comic scenes of pantomime it is not unusual to see a very small child, dressed, perhaps, as a charity boy, crossing the stage bearing in his hand a slice of bread and butter. The clown steals this article of food and devours it. Whereupon the child, crying aloud, pursues him hither and thither about the stage. The incident always excites much amusement, for in pantomime the world is turned upside down and moral principals have no existence. Cruelty is only comical and outrageous crimes the best of jokes. The paper parcel borne to the theatre by the clown under mention, enclosed the bread and butter that was to figure in the harlequinade.

"You see, I'm a particular feeder," the performer explained. "I can't eat bread and butter of anyone's cutting. Besides, I've tried it, and they only afford salt butter. I can't stand that. So as I've got to eat it and no mistake, with all the house looking at me, I cut a slice when I'm having my own tea at home and bring it down with me."

Rather among the refreshments of the side wings than of the stage must be counted that reeking hot tumbler of "very brown, very hot, and very strong brandy and water," which, as Doctor Doran relates, was prepared for poor Edmund Kean, as, towards the close of his career, he was wont to stagger from before the footlights, and overcome by his exertion and infirmities, to sink, "a helpless, speechless, fainting, bent up mass," into the chair placed in readiness to receive the shattered, ruined actor. With Kean's prototype in acting and excess, George Frederick Cooke, it was less a question of stage or side wing refreshments than of the measure of preliminary potation he had indulged in. In what state would he come down to the theatre? Upon the answer to that inquiry the entertainment of the night greatly depended.

"I was drunk the night before last," Cooke said on one occasion. "Still, I acted and they hissed me. Last night I was drunk again, and I didn't act. They hissed all the same. There's no knowing how to please the public."

A fine actor, Cooke was also a genuine humorist; and it must be said for him, although a like excuse has been too often pleaded for such failings as his, that his senses gave way and his brain became affected after very slight indulgence. From this, however, he could not be persuaded to abstain, and so made havoc of his genius and terminated, prematurely and ignobly enough, his professional career.

Many stories are extant as to performances being interrupted by the entry of innocent messengers, bringing to the players, in the presence of the audience, refreshments they had designed to consume behind the scenes, or sheltered from observation between the wings. Thus it is told of one Walls, who was the prompter in a Scottish theatre, and occasionally appeared in minor parts, that he once directed a maid-of-all-work, employed in the wardrobe department of the theatre, to bring him a gill of whiskey. The night was wet, so the girl, not caring to go out, entrusted the commission to a little boy who happened to be standing by. The play was "Othello" and Walls played the Duke. The scene of the senate was in course of representation.

Brabantio had just stated, "My particular grief is of no floodgate and o'erbearing nature, that it engulfs and swallows other sorrows, and it is still itself,"

And the Duke, obedient to his cue, had inquired, "Why, what's the matter?"

When the little boy appeared on the stage bearing a pewter measure, and exclaimed, "It's just the whiskey, Mr. Walls. And I could na git only a fourpence, so yer awn the landlord a penny. And he says it's time you was payin' what's doon i' the book."

The senate broke up amidst the uproarious laughter of the audience.

[*New York Clipper*, November 16, 1872]

STAGE MISHAPS
by Susan Archer Weiss

The importance to a play of well ordered and well managed accessories is admitted by those who understand the subject. Not alone is it necessary that the actors have thoroughly mastered their parts, but the greatest care must be bestowed upon the minor details surrounding them. Otherwise, a single flaw or imperfection in the adjuncts is apt to destroy in the mind of the spectator the impression of the most perfect acting, and not infrequently to convert the heroic into the ludicrous. Indeed, it may be asserted that in no other situation is the saying about the close connection of the sublime and the ridiculous more capable of illustration than on the stage, as there are few more situations liable to accident or misadventure calculated to produce this effect. As examples, I can recall several instances which have come under my own observation or that of my friends.

On one occasion when Mrs. Mowatt was playing in one of her favorite characters, she turned, and with a bewitching smile presented a small basket of flowers to her lover. The basket had been hastily and carelessly packed with some green market stuff as a basis for the surface layer of flowers; and in the act of transferring it, some roses caught in the light tissue of her dress and fell out, dragging with them an unmistakably large cabbage leaf. Thenceforth, the beauty and the pathos of the act were lost upon the audience, who could see only the unromantic vegetable lying at the feet of the fair performer.

Some twenty or more years ago in Richmond, Va., Miss _____ was playing Pauline in "The Lady of Lyons." With clasped hands, uplifted eyes, and tender, impassioned utterance, she was in the act of saying to the unrecognized Claude, "Tell him, for years I never nursed a thought that was not his; that on his wandering way, daily and nightly, poured a mourner's prayers." When suddenly, from behind the scenes [there] rolled an immense watermelon. Slowly and deliberately bowling across the stage, it struck the actress' feet, causing her to start and hastily move aside. [It] then disappeared in the orchestra. Pauline recovered her presence of mind and, with only some slight faltering, proceeded with her tender speech; to which the heartless Claude listened with most unsentimental signs of amusement, which he strove in vain to conceal behind the chapeau which he held in his hand.

About the time of this occurrence "The Castles of the Seven Passions" had a great run in the same city of Richmond. One night, while preparing for the sudden transformation scene from hut to palace, the slat partition gave way, and a man in shirt sleeves was unceremoniously precipitated into the presence of the lovers and of the audience. On another occasion, not long after, during the performance of "Mazeppa", a pile of rocks fell, revealing a man (one of the scene shifters) snatching a hurried refreshment of a bread and cheese sandwich and a glass of beer.

A friend of mine attended a play wherein a fearful tempest was symbolized by lightning from above and peals of thunder, while in the distance a ship was seen tossed upon the sea. The thunder was produced partly by means of a wheelbarrow containing cannon balls, trundled briskly at intervals up and down a sloping plank crossed with wooden bars. Unfortunately, the barrow tripped and was overturned, and the balls performed a lively race across the stage, while the actors hopped and skipped about, and the musicians, though mostly fat Germans, exhibited some remarkable feats of agility in avoiding the unexpected hailstorm. To add to the absurdity of the spectacle, the ship had all this time remained perfectly still and becalmed in the midst of a raging sea. And now a meteor fell suddenly from heaven, snapping and fizzing in a manner to greatly astonish and perplex philosophers. The actors, making no pretense to philosophy, rushed off the stage, whilst the manager himself rushed on it, armed with a broom, before which the mysterious meteor and aerolyte disappeared.

Many who read this will remember the beautiful Celeste, and how like a veritable angel she appeared in ascending on seraph wings into the mysterious regions beyond the stage. It was my fortune to see her thus ascending, waving a graceful parting *adieu* to the adoring mortals below; when, lo! a rope fell from heaven and sheared off one of the glittering pinions of the seraph.

I have heard a venerable relative of mine tell how, in 1811 or 1812, a then famous actor was one night playing Macbeth in Norfolk, Va., when a tame monkey by some means got on the stage and concealed himself behind some drapery. Here he remained till the combat with Macduff; when he flew out, darted about the stage, and jumped up and down, chattering in the greatest terror and distress. The fighting heroes could with difficulty preserve their gravity, and some of the audience yelled with laughter.

I have witnessed in public exhibitions accidents as amusing as any I have witnessed on the stage. Of this character was the upsetting of the boat in which the Lady of Shalotte, lying waxen pale upon her flowery bier, was being borne "down to towered Camelot." The indignation of the suddenly revived corpse was most ludicrous to behold. Again, at the long time ago "Eruption of Vesuvius", the fearful mountain in the distance suddenly sank down and the head of a monstrous, red-faced, begrimed giant was for an instant visible, protruding from the smoking crater.

When Rosser's two magnificent paintings of Adam and Eve were on exhibition through the South, my enjoyment of them was once very materially interfered with by overhearing a sharp dispute between a colored lady and gentleman behind me as to whether that famous apple was a "sheephead" or an "Albemarle pippin." Also, the lady insisted that she saw "lettuces growing under the apple tree"; to which her lord responded by inquiring in great distrust "whether she didn't know that it was only after the fall that Adam took to raising garden truck."

But the scene of all others which caused me the most intense amusement (I was only sixteen at the time.) was during the famous traveling exhibition of "The Burning of Moscow." The scene opened beautifully, [with] lights gleaming and moving here and there, the moon slowly rising, gilded tower and mosque-like pinnacle; then a lurid blaze of fire shooting up into the dark blue sky, towers falling, the doomed city in flames, the van of the French army crossing the great bridge in retreat. At length the climax of interest was reached when it was announced that Napoleon and his staff were in sight. On they came over the majestic bridge (the great Emperor on his snow white horse), slow, dignified, majestic. Suddenly the horse reared on his hind legs, stood a moment trembling, then made several hops and jumps forward. He then planted his forefeet firmly and lifted his heels in the air, his rider lying flat on his neck. No one noticed them. The long train of tall grenadiers and white baggage wagons marched stoically past their great commander. Presently, the horse again started on his hind legs, progressing in spasmodic leaps, whilst the great Emperor lay serenely back on the crupper, with his heels high in the air. By this time his staff seemed to become conscious of the extraordinary situation. There was an abrupt pause, a sensation, a trembling commotion; and I saw a long staff projected from the end of the bridge (a contrivance of the enemy, doubtless) which struck down the white war horse into a more natural position, and then, with repeated blows on the back of the great Napoleon drove, that conquering hero forward across the bridge. But evidently this indignity had aroused his heroic spirit, for he now betrayed symptoms of intense ire. He charged at his staff, laid them right and left; then, pushing through them, conscious of victory, again lay serenely on his back, with his feet in the air, and so finally disappeared over the bridge of Moscow.

[*New York Clipper*, June 23, 1877]

ACCIDENTS IN THEATRES

Dion Boucicault has had a great deal of experience among various theatres in this and in the old country, and his opinions on matters connected with the stage are entitled to much consideration. The increase in the number of accidents which have of late taken place in England has called forth the following article from the fertile brain of Mr. Boucicault; and as it contains some facts and suggestions which may be of service on this side of the Atlantic, we give it publicity.

"Public attention has been drawn to the necessity of providing against accidents in theatres. It is proposed to afford protection on the stage to performers, especially to the ballet girls, and a ready egress for the audience in case of alarm. The London managers, at a meeting convened by the Lord Chamberlain, agreed very unanimously that the accidents which have lately occurred to the ballet girls were wholly attributable to their carelessness; but if the ballet had been favored with a similar interview, they would, with equal unanimity and justice, also have attributed the blame to the managers. The gas arrangements on the stage are defective and dangerous. The ground light, as it is termed, is an iron gas tube which lies on the stage, and is supplied by a flexible pipe passing through the stage to a gas joint below. This ground light is tapped for burners at every twelve inches, and the burners employed are of two kinds: the ordinary fishtail or common open burner, and the Argand or circular burner, which requires a glass chimney. These latter give the best light and are essential when blue or red tints are required, an effect produced by the use of colored glass chimneys.

"These Argand burners in the ground light are the principal cause of the mischief. A ballet girl's skirts come to her knee, being about eighteen inches from the ground. If she stood over a row of fishtail burners, her skirts would not ignite at that distance; but if she stood for an instant over a row of Argands, the heat and fire conducted by the glass chimney will set her petticoats on fire instantly. It is worse than foolish to say that these lights are protected by a low parapet of scenery called a ground row, sometimes, but rarely, eighteen inches in height. The managers know very well that the skirts of the ballet are so short, and project so far from the figure, that if a girl stands within two feet of this ground row her petticoats will clear it and extend over the gaslights beyond. It is equally cruel and vain to say that the girls have been warned not to step over these lights; they know very well that it is exceedingly rare for a ballet girl to attempt such a feat as to step over a row of Argand burners.

"The accident occurs thus: when the stage is crowded, and on the entrance of the principals, the ballet are moved back, and thus one girl pushes and crowds upon another; and as they are thus forced backwards with their faces kept towards the public, how is the poor girl in the back row to know when her skirts get into danger?

"These Argand burners in ground rows should be prohibited. It will be a severe deprivation to the painter, who clings fondly to the effect they produce, but there is no help for it. A wire gauze will protect a row of fishtails, but it is no protection to a row of Argands, the fire and heat from which will penetrate the guard. All side lights, standard lights, wing lights and battens should, whether furnished with rows of single jets, or fishtails, or Argands, be guarded with a network of wire, of a mesh not larger than one inch square.

"The managers complain that the ballet girls will not make their ballet skirts of the uninflamable muslin, and they can find no means of compelling them to do so. I can find a means. Let the managers supply the ballet with the skirts as well as the upper dress. These skirts cost about 18s. per girl--no great outlay in theatres where the pantomime costs from £1,000 to £2,000 to get up. It is true that the girls are very thoughtless, and perhaps life at 15s. a week, or 18s. at most, with silk stockings, satin shoes, and ballet skirts to find out of it, is not so precious a consideration as it might be; but they are very young and not accustomed to much consideration from anyone, and, therefore, grow indifferent to their own welfare.

"The precautions taken with the view to secure egress for the public in the case of fire are excellent in theory, but I venture to affirm would be found totally insufficient in practice. Great stress is laid on the necessity of escape staircases and escape doors. Drury Lane Theatre is quite a curiosity in this respect, and when I was manager of the establishment I had many an entertaining ramble in those catacombs. Is it possible that any practical or reflecting man can for a moment entertain the idea that a single person in a panic-stricken crowd would avail himself of an unknown and mysterious staircase leading no one knows whither? It has been my misfortune to witness more than one serious alarm of fire in a crowded theatre. The impulse of the audience is invariably the same. The men are too quick and the women too slow to move, but they all make instinctively for the door at which they have entered. They neither hear nor see; but panic blind and panic deaf, they will take no other means of escape. A door may be opened beside them with a palpable egress, and they will not see it, nor can they be made to see it. They only know one way out, and that is the way they came in; they have no confidence or trust in any other. This is very unreasonable, very foolish, very absurd; but it is the fact. An escaping man will rather jump out of a window twenty feet high, where he sees his risk, than enter a staircase or corridor with the issue of which he is unacquainted. All the staircases and corridors of Drury Lane Theatre, wide and spacious as they are, would be found to be useless for the purpose for which they were designed. It is not there the mischief would occur; it is in the first narrow doorway between the auditorium and those fine corridors. Here some poor woman faints and falls down; next those behind her are forced over her; and thus a pile of human beings blocks the doorway in a moment. The obstruction increases the panic of those behind, who jam the mass all the more inextricable. A similar accident might occur in Drury Lane Theatre in the elbow passage leading from the dressing corridor to the grand staircase.

"It would be manifestly very unfair to interfere with the theaters in an arbitrary manner by refusing a license to such as could not show a fully efficient egress for the audience in case of alarm. In the large theatres the entrances are complicated, spacious here and pinched there; while in the smaller houses the entrances are narrow. They all want simplicity and straightforwardness in design. But if the mischief is built in, and cannot be cured in the manner proposed, the next precaution should be to provide a method for preventing the affrighted crowd from sacrificing themselves; this should be in the form of an impediment to the rush. There is not a theatre in London, however defectively built, where the largest audience it ever contained might not readily clear out of it in five minutes; and there never has happened in any building an instance of a fire which has gained any important hold on the structure under twenty minutes or half an hour.

"Practically speaking, then, as theatres are, it is not so necessary to provide extra and supplementary means of egress as to contrive some method of resisting the first panic rush of an affrighted crowd, and obliging them to go out slowly. The late accident in Chili exemplifies my experience remarkably. Here was a large area on the ground floor; the door was large, so large that, although blocked up with bodies, a man was able to throw his lasso over the mass into the church and drag out a human being. There were also side doors of escape, of which very small avail was made. But the affrighted crowd acted as they invariably do--they rushed to the entrance door. Some woman fainted. She created a block. And thus the egress, which was ample, was obstructed; and had it been twice or thrice the size, it would have been blocked. But I feel assured if the church had been divided into pews, and thus an obstacle created to massing a crowd, not a single life would have been sacrificed.")

[*New York Clipper*, May 28, 1864]

BEHIND THE SCENES

There are a few people not connected with theatrical life who, being lovers of the drama, do not long sometimes to peep at the mimic world behind the gaudy scenes, and see the actor as he is, divested of his paint and professional garb. The player lives in such a strange world that we build up around him a pretty, romantic idea, and fall down and worship that creation of our own fancy; until, viewing him as he is, and seeing with our own eyes the toilsome, weary life he leads, [and] the peculiar, many temptations he has, we come to know that he is but a man as ourselves, with the same feelings, the same aspirations.

Few actors off the stage like to talk shop to outsiders. Few of them carry the dust of the stage about with them in these modern days. It has been my fortune to have known and associated with a large number of these gentry. They have their faults and bad practices like other professional men; they sometimes ruin themselves by drink and riot; they are often careless of a good name and reckless of the future; they are but men, like other men, "a mixture of the angel and the devil."

I have often thought, as I have stood at the prompter's table, or whiled away an hour in the green-room, or talked at the "wings," as the play was going on in front, with some stage king in his royal robes, or young Hamlet in his "inky cloak," that if the public, who were weeping before the footlights at the portrayal of dramatic wrong and misery and sorrow, could hear the remarks made by the actors themselves on the play, or [see] the utter indifference they show just the moment they pass out of sight of the audience, they would save some of the feeling and sympathy for the sorrowing ones of real life, and not waste so much on these empty creatures of the drama. When seeing the play from behind it generally seems ridiculous to hear an audience thunder applause, or sob by the bucket-full, or go into convulsions of laughter, when the hard, forced art which produces it is plain to your sight, causing a feeling of disgust. Booth was playing the sombre "Stranger" one night at his theatre (and usually effective, too), and the brilliant audience were "taking on" in a wild way. He came off from his powerful scene, where the Stranger refuses to give the two children to their mother's care, and stood leaning against the wing watching Mrs. Farron personate the broken hearted mother. It is a tearful scene and plenty of tears were being shed in front.

With a queer smile, Booth turned to my companion and myself and said, "I wonder what the audience think of this piece? Mrs. Haller, I take it, was nothing but a common woman of the town; and the Stranger a confounded fool for not being glad he was well rid of her."

And in a moment afterwards the great actor was on the stage again, deep in his part, with a sad, dejected face, and tender, sorrowing words. Powerful indeed is art! I have seen actors come from the delivery of some fearfully passionate outbursts, in which it would seem as if every nerve of their nature was put, and coolly join in a merry dance that was going on in the green-room. There is no sentiment behind the scenes. Acting is business; and as business, the art is put into it. When it is finished, the actor drops right down from his stilts and becomes himself.

There is one good little story I will tell before taking my readers behind the scenes at Niblo's during a late performance of "The White Fawn," which I started out in this sketch to do. A well known piece had been running at a Broadway theatre for some weeks to the delight of the town. The villain of it was performed by one of the best New York actors. After passing through a series of stage rascality, the ruffian is brought up by a round turn and lodged in a prison which opens into a courtyard secured by a frowning wall. As the play goes on, the prisoner bursts his prison door, removes his fetters by means of a file he had concealed, climbs the wall, and is just about to make his escape when the guards rush in, fire and mortally wound him, and he staggers to the footlights and dies in the most approved melodramatic manner, the death scene being a great point in the play. One night the stage manager had either failed to provide the soldiers who rush in and do the killing, or they had gone round the corner for their beer and forgotten their duty. The prisoner cautiously breaks the door of his cell, and, taking to the stage, files the irons from his feet; and, absorbed in his part, [he] did not notice the guard were not standing at the wing ready for the cue. With the words, "Ah! the irons are off. I am free once more!" he hastily ascends the wall, and, nearing the top, says the words at which the cruel shot was expected to be fired. But no shot came. He gave a side glance to the wing and saw no soldiers. He must die. He must not go over the wall. Quick as a flash he saw the need of doing something. So giving an exclamation of fright, he falls from the wall and reels to the front, saying, "Oh, horrible! I have swallowed the file!" and dies in a most approved fit of strangulation. And strange to say, the audience took it all in good part and the piece was finished to their satisfaction.

The stage entrance to Niblo's Theatre is on Crosby Street, just back of Broadway. Going through a narrow, covered porchway, you are admitted directly upon the stage. The dressing rooms are situated above and below, taking in a part of the rear of the Metropolitan Hotel, steep stairways going to them from the sides of the stage. During the week "The White Fawn" was on the boards and every available space was occupied by the ballet. The performers and the extensive machinery used in the piece made it a difficult matter to get around inside the scenes, [due to the congestion of] properties, or tripping in the way of some muslin divinity of the ballet, or falling over the tail of some "demon" just ready to go on for the scene. The prompter's table was the only safe place; and there I watched the piece through one night.

It was an hour before the curtain rose that I arrived behind the scenes. The stage was set for the beautiful picture of "King Ding Dong's Palace." A rehearsal of a new figure for the dance was in progress, as a number of green girls had been placed in the ballet, who were to be drilled into shape. Carpenters were nailing scenes and making all the noise they could with their hammers. The gas men were working their calcium lights to see if they were in order. The captain of the "supes" was giving loud orders to his men and putting some fresh arrivals through their paces. The actors were gathering, dressed for their characters. And towards the front stood the patient ballet master, trying to make grace and ease where nature had scorned to put any, trying to make feet turn out instead of persisting in turning in, and ungainly limbs assume correct positions as the figures of the dance demanded. There were a score or more of girls around him in pretty, short dresses, chatting like a flock of blackbirds and doing everything but what the little Frenchman wanted them to do. When he counted the third change they would be finishing the second or the fourth. When he marked a backward movement for them, woman-like, they would go the other way. They seemed to take as much delight in teasing and bothering Monsieur as if he had been a lover or a husband. His patience gave way at last and he swore a few French oaths, I am sorry to say; but they were heeded, and more pains taken.

There had to be a constant change in the ordinary ballet girls during the run of "The White Fawn." Going over the same things night after night made the girls very disgusted, and they would drop out of the ranks in dozens every week. Their places having to be filled by others made frequent rehearsals necessary and untold work for the ballet master. Every motion, pose, evolution, had to be practiced hour after hour before the graceful and charming groupings that the public saw could be presented in a fit shape.

Oh, how the girls in the piece did keep up a continual running fire of talk! After the play began one could hardly hear two words out of five for the noise of their tongues. Every few minutes somebody had to be sent to stop them. They would collect in their dressing rooms and talk, behind the flats out of the way, talk, talk, talk, and even when on the stage or at the wing preparing to go on not a moment did they seem to "let up" in their machine-like chatter. There were over a hundred of them engaged in the piece and they were the most troublesome things in it. Scold them and they would laugh, be harsh with them and they would break out into a cry and leave the piece in the lurch. They were not to be tamed down to order. They were girls and they meant to be girls and the manager couldn't make anything else of them but silly chatterboxes who were bound to do as they pleased.

"I didn't sleep nights," said the worthy stage manager, "because of the fuss I have we these girls. They wear the life out of me."

What a queer old place it is, to be sure, behind the scenes of a theatre! How the actors can ever take the illusion and sentiment of the play in the midst of so much disenchanting material I often wonder. In private study they may soar to the ideal conceptions of the poet, but on the bare, dreary, dingy stage, where everything is false and unreal, I should think every fancy would fly from them.

On every side are stacks of scenes to be used in the play. Some are painted on both sides, and representing a fairy grotto and a demon's cavern with strange inconsistency. They are grimy with the prints of the scene shifter's hands. They are torn in some places and patched in others. There stands a golden throne made of rough planks, and, like many other things in this world, with its best side turned out. Here are heaps of stage properties of such names and appearance it is impossible for an outsider to tell for what purpose they are used. There are dragons' tails, heads of fishes, drinking cups, wreaths of gay, impossible flowers, gilt crosses, badges for knights, trappings soiled and faded, dishes of fruit which require unbounded imagination to decide what they are meant for, red hot pokers for the funny man, which lie quite harmless now and don't even scorch the faces by their side--all stage deceptions which the audience will take as real as the play goes on. There are some "mossy banks," upon which bright, sunny beings will recline. They are rude boards covered with painted cloth, and are as hard as a brick to the touch. How I pity the poor girls in thin dresses who will do the reclining!

Talking in groups are fairies and mortals (princes); King Ding Dong, an evil looking monster with great, glaring eyes; the wicked grandmother of the Princess and the angelic daughter of the King with her; carpenters in work dress with beings clad in rich armor and splendid suits; my Lord Chamberlain is taking a bite of a ham sandwich and a glass of lager, and casting soft glances at a pretty ballet girl coming down the stage in a delicate pink muslin dress; the stage manager is flying here and there, giving his orders in a decided tone. All is ready at last. The orchestra has struck into the air for the curtain. The prompter's bell rings. "Clear the stage, ladies and gentlemen!" The din of the bells commence. The curtain rises slowly. The house is quiet and "The White Fawn" begins.

It takes away all pleasure to see a piece of this kind from behind. Some of the finest effects seen from the audience are tame and insipid seen so close. Some of the finest women are really ugly. Can that bold, ungainly, hard-faced, pitted, frowning woman, who is exercising her limbs so freely at the flats and getting herself into trim before she appears before the crowded house, be the sylph-like beauty whom we were wont to applaud with enthusiasm? She don't smile now, and her maid hasn't touched her face yet with "Email de Paris," and put on the beauty spots. By and by she will glide down the stage to sweet music, wearing a fascinating smile, and have flowers thrown at her. She will captivate somebody then with her elegant face and form and dress.

Are the gorgeous scenes which we thought such a paragon of art these dirty daubs, covered with Dutch metal and floss, course and wretched and shabby--the waterfall which looked so real, and sparkled so prettily, this muslin thing that a stout man in shirt sleeves is turning up and down, while overhead a gas man is directing his light upon it-- these dresses, these armors, the gay processions and pageants, are they nothing but such cheap displays as this? All fancy goes in seeing art laid out so naked.

Everything goes by rule. The prompter touches his bell and the machinery does its work. Traps open and close, men are pulling at ropes, and other men are fastening scenes and pulling up supports. The actors on the stage are whispering jokes to each other, or talking in low tones about the "house"--the money there is in it--during the time they were not engaged in the dialogue, or off the stage drinking beer, reading the *Clipper*, or in the green-room taking a nap or playing a quiet game of poker or whist until the call boy summons them again to duty. They have gone over their roles so many times it has ceased to interest them. As one or two get through their parts they hastily change the stage dress, wash off the rouge, and dash out into the street as if relieved.

And the ladies, costumed in character, are parading before great mirrors, getting up elegant attitudes or bringing their dresses to a proper and graceful swing. They are studying expressions, too, in the glass--how to look at such portions of the play that may call for some particular effect, how to put on these tender and head-turning airs that captivate an audience and send many a youth in front home to dream of [them] in a wild, feverish delirium.

Here is a constant bustle of change as act by act goes by. The ballet change their dresses a half dozen times. After a fatiguing ballet some of the great "stars" will come panting and heated from the stage and sink down into a seat almost exhausted. But the encore will sound, and a maid will brush a little powder on their faces, smooth their dresses and, gathering up her strength, the *prima danseuse* will bound onto the stage again, smiling and bewitching. I have known these women to come from a night's work so pale and weary that they would lie for an hour in their dressing rooms, too tired to change their stage clothes. And yet, they go through the toil long months with wonderful spirit. It is not strange that one by one they drop into early graves. The principal artists are paid large sums, but the labor is extremely hard.

That the actor's life is unnatural and severe none can realize who do not see it behind the scenes. There is nothing to cheer and elevate the hopes save in the approval the public give. And even if a player does his best, and "plays many parts" well, on the morrow a cold shoulder may be turned to him by his patrons, and his hopes [may be] crushed to the dust.

[*New York Clipper*, September 12, 1868]

PART III: ABOUT SOME AUDIENCES

✾

IN THE AUDIENCE
by W. E. M.

Mirabel does justice to a first night in words of rapture that Charles Lamb long afterward might have used. But to the proper observer there are two plays in the theatre of an evening--that which is performed on the stage and that which enacts itself extemporaneously in the audience. To enjoy all of the latter, I have ever made it a rule to go early, for sometimes a very interesting prologue takes place at the doors. The sight of the motley crowd squeezing up to the box office, the bustling there, the paying out of the admission money, the disputes with the uncompromising ticket seller (who is favorably the most rigidly imperturbable of human beings), the rush for programs, the choice of seats form altogether an exhibition not to be witnessed anywhere else.

The arm chairs now in use are inventions, it must be granted, most invaluable. Everybody has his allowance of space and the surety of not being intruded upon. Once settled in your throne, you feel pretty safe. All that you have now to dread is an unpleasant neighbor. How closely you eye each person who passes down the aisle. But your primary horror is of that inevitable old gentleman who attends the theatre but seldom and is consequently ignorant of its rules. He begins his evening by tormenting the usher. He dawdles down to the front of the orchestra; and, notwithstanding he sees "taken" staring him in the face all around, he sinks into the choicest spot he can find. Usher touches him on the arm several times and at last only attracts his attention by giving him a violent nudge.

"All these places are secured, sir. If you haven't a coupon for the orchestra you must go further back."

"I paid 75 cents," reasons the old gentleman. "They told me that would take me all over the house."

"But these seats are taken. You pay a dollar for these."

"But they told me at the door 75 cents. . ."

"Yes, but a certain space is always reserved in advance at an additional charge. You must move back."

"At the door," persists the unconquerable old person, "they said 75 cents. . ."

Usher leads him off by force, but is by no means rid of him yet. He can't be suited elsewhere with any accommodation whatever. He moves here and there, falling over peoples legs, knocking down umbrellas and hats, hunting for programs; and makes himself the object of more profanity that should fall to the lot of any human being in the world on a single day.

The drunken man is the next nuisance. First of all, he poisons the surrounding atmosphere with the exhalations of thoroughly moistened skin. He uses very bad language, to the interruptions of your hearing of the play. He leans on the seat before him and blows his breath down the back of the lady sitting there. He is continually staggering out for more refreshment and coming back again just when you think he has left for good. Finally, he gets very drunk and raises a disturbance. This necessitates his expulsion; and, as the officers are carrying him away, he struggles and wipes his muddy boots all over your coat and alarms you, perhaps, by brandishing a loaded revolver.

The third nuisance is that accommodating creature, the communicative man. He has seen the play before several times, knows it by heart in fact. He supplies you with a summary of the action before the curtain rises. He tells you in advance what everybody on the stage is going to do next. He repeats, with great exactness, the dialogue of the performers as it progresses. He helps to work up the climax; and, just as you are wondering with intense interest what the catastrophe will be, he hurries to your relief by explaining all.

I remember, years ago, when I first saw "The Ticket of Leave Man" performed, one of these agreeable persons was sitting by me; and at the time when Hawkshaw enters disguised as the navy--when, in short, I was in an exquisite fever of suspense, not suspecting in the remotest degree the turn of the plot--this pleasant neighbor of mine revealed the startling *denouement* with an expression of happiness in being able to serve me that no words could describe. I threw my arms around his neck and cursed him till I couldn't utter another oath.

The fourth nuisance is the stranger who has no program and is not acquainted with the names of the actors. He asks a question every instant. If a performer leaves the stage but two minutes, when he returns, the stranger, with a fresh show of interest, whispers, "And who is this?" So it goes till, in desperation, you sing out at each appearance, with the monotony of habit, "Here's Wallack. This is Gilbert. Now comes Rockwell. And Fisher is entering." till the curtain falls.

But defend me from the fifth nuisance, the man [that's] hard of hearing. He leans forward with both hands at his ears and seems to be growing into the very stage itself. Yet for all, he never fails to miss the points. He perceives the audience roaring suddenly and, in dreadful agitation, he turns to you, who are rapt in following the speech, and asks, "What was that? What was that?" If you are not a madman by the end of the play you must have settle wits indeed.

Then there is the country family refreshing themselves with apples and peanuts every minute. They are disposed very near you and when the paternal head goes out to renew stock, which he does regularly every act, he always feels it his duty to tread on your toes. And so they sit grinding and crunching and talking and smelling of stables and stale cake and a damp umbrella, until your pleasure is nullified for that evening.

Next is the unpleasant impostor, the man who knows all the performers by their first names. Though in reality he has no more personal acquaintance with the parties whom he speaks of so familiarly than yourself, he persists in a nomenclature that would have you believe him their most intimate friend. He tells you what advice he gave "Johnny" Mortimer about his wig, how he instructed Joe Folk as to the business of a scene in Captain Absolute. He narrates the joke he played off on "Ned" Booth. He has also a capital story to tell about himself and "Dan" Harkins. And he does not omit the account of his first meeting with "Jim" Wallack and "Lem" Shewell. These scamps are not always the perpetrators of harmless lies, as I know in my own experience with one. On one occasion, he told me, with the most amazing minuteness, of a great service he had once done for a very popular actress whose performance we were then witnessing. Now, I happen to be a particular acquaintance of the lady's. The matter was of much delicacy and she was a woman whose timidity in dealing with the everyday world was actually morbid. Consequently, I was thoroughly satisfied that the assertion of my familiar friend was an atrocious falsehood;

and I was just provoked enough to tax him with it. Seeing himself caught, he smiled a very childlike smile and admitted that he had been drawing on his inventive powers; but only, he added, to furnish food for conversation.

But there are many nuisances in an audience besides these enumerated here. The tobacco man, who goes out to smoke between every act and floods the floor the remainder of the time, is a nuisance. The man with the bad cold, who barks by your ear every two seconds, is another. The stupid man, who can't make out what the performance is about, is another. The man who is restless and yawns continually is still another. And, in brief, they are endless.

[*New York Clipper*, November 4, 1871]

THE BOWERY GODS: THEIR WAYS AND FAVORITES
by Frank McHale

A visit to the gods of the Bowery is one of the most delightful and quaintest things in creation. A person cannot imagine what queer sights he will behold at catching a first glimpse of them. The following description has been written by one who for years has been a close observer of their manners; and people familiar with the habits and customs of these uncultured yet natural critics of the drama will quickly recognize them by this little sketch. To any skeptic who doubts what is written here and wishes to honor these gods with a visit, yet is unacquainted with the way to reach them, the authentic account beneath, compiled from official sources, may prove advantageous.

Attached to the theatre is an entrance over which is painted in black letters that grand and expressive word suggesting the glories of ancient Rome during the reign of the pagan emperors---"Amphitheatre." On one side of the passageway leading to the place just spoken of is situated a small room, which is used for a boxoffice. The interior part of it is decorated with pictures of sensational plays and portraits of professional celebrities. Ned Stetson, with his grave face and profile features, and likewise Zoe, with beaming eyes and curly hair, occupy prominent niches in this vast art collection.

Tickets can be had of genial Joe Young, who reigns supreme here; and flatters himself with the idea that he can sling more pasteboard in five minutes than an ordinary ticket seller can get away with in a quarter of an hour. After purchasing tickets, the next thing on the program is to ascend the long and spiral staircase. Do not be alarmed if the ascent is not finished after a reasonable time has elapsed. Remember that perserverence eventually triumphs, and keep on mounting steadily upward until "the brain begins to swim, and the eyes grow heavy and dim." You will then come in sight of the ticket taker, who politely extends his hand for your piece of pasteboard. This gentleman is known amongst the deities by the Teutonic appellation of "Dutch." A few steps more usher you into the saloon, where the gods quaff ambrosial nectar and munch peanuts and pig's feet.

By entering one of the doors which lead into the amphitheatre, you can behold the objects of your curiosity. A low, humming noise greets the ear and the familiar cry of "Lemonade, apples, peanuts!" pervades the entire atmosphere. The lights are down, as the performance has not yet begun. By walking around to the side and gazing down below you will notice that the dress circle and balconies are filled with ladies and gentlemen; but as they shall prove of no interest whatsoever, you must devote your whole and undivided attention to the gods. They are rapidly assembling and becoming rather noisy and loquacious. One of them asks his companion, who is probably a newsboy or a bootblack, "if the old man is drunk tonight" and "how much money did he give the old woman?" They are also getting somewhat impatient and express that impatience by the incessant tramping of their feet. Queries are anxiously passed between them, such as, "Will they ever h'ist the rag?" and "Isn't it time for musicianers to come out?"

The bell suddenly twinkles and the lights go up. The gods send forth a shout of joy at this welcome fore running of what is coming. The musicians, headed by the portly Dean, emerge from beneath the stage and take their respective places in the orchestra. After fumbling a few minutes with their sheet music and testing anon their instruments to the undisguised disgust of the gods, the leader's tap is heard, and the overture commences. When it is concluded, the bell tinkles again and the curtain rises to appropriate music.

The gods become very excited as the play progresses. Every noble sentiment uttered is acknowledged by them with deafening plaudits. If the two emissaries in the service of the heavy villain are seen creeping cautiously over to the spot where the virtuous hero in the play stands, unconscious of his impending peril, loud cries of warning come from them, something like "Cheese it, Kiggy! Bounce them!" And when the curtain is descending on some thrilling tableau, wild cheers and piercing whistles resound through the theatre, and criticisms are indulged in in loud tones.

"I say, Mickey," calls out one of the deities, "what do you think of Winter?"

"Red hot!" cries Mickey.

"Hey, Jimmy!" cries another, "how's Marston and Lou Sylvester?"

"I tell yer what, young feller, them two is bang up!"

"Sa-ay, Lemonade!" yells a third in a rather sarcastic manner. This young gentleman is addressing his speech to the humble vender of that delicious beverage. "Gimme a two cent glass, and cussed quick, too, d'ya hear?"

"Ain't got any two cent glasses," responds Lemonade curtly.

The gods are always delighted to behold their favorites and they regret exceedingly their departure from the boards. On Joe Winter's farewell night they went perfectly wild. Loud and continued applause greeted his every entrance on the stage. At the termination of the play he made an impromptu speech in which he bade the ladies and gentlemen farewell. But his last words [were] to the gods, and those words seemed to come from the heart. [They] were, "Goodbye, boys!"

When the good natured face and robust figure of Ned Marston appear, the welcome they give him is terrific. Ned acknowledges it good humoredly and after the storm subsides he takes up his cue and proceeds with his part. The gods never forget what is due to Mrs. Jones, the accomplished leading lady of the theatre for many years. She is an established favorite, and they like her acting. The moment Louise Sylvester bounds upon the stage the Marston excitement revives, for this little lady is also a great favorite with the gods.

This strange ilk is composed of newsboys, bootblacks and a slight sprinkling of lads who work at trades. It is the only real amusement they have to while away a few hours in the friendly interior of "Old Drury." Poor fellows! Some of them suffer hard usage from drunken and dissipated parents; and if the pleasures of the theatre were denied them, they might, perhaps, seek worse places.

[*New York Clipper*, June 20, 1874]

THE "GODS"
by J. Booth Renauld

Since there have been actors and since there have been people to witness acting, the "gods" of the pit and of the gallery have been an individualized class among theatre-goers. An erroneous impression prevails among the theatrically uninitiated, and even in the minds of some of the occasional frequenters of places of amusements, that the class sub-denominated or deified as "gods" is composed exclusively of boot-blacks and newsboys. These latter personages undoubtedly comprise a large number of them, but the ranks of the "gods" are not exclusively filled by them. On the contrary, therein are a class of overgrown boys--young men even--who would be more properly termed "roughs," and these have largely contributed to giving the "gods" the reputation of being "boisterous, low and vulgar."

In England the character of the latter for obstreperousness was long held as being far above that of their prototypes in our midst; but this superiority has never been rightfully claimed since there was a Chatham Theatre, or since the Thespian temple of the Bowery and its Broadway counterpart came into existence. There, as here, newsboys and bootblacks are the best behaved among the deified class, though this is, perhaps, not advancing much.

Strange as it may appear, they are also the most respectable, notwithstanding that they have been attacked by some reverend individual who could not see anybody but knights of the brush and box and their *confrères* of the newspaper in the throng, who usually evince their impatience at the tardy rising of the curtain by shouting, "Up with the rag!" and have given occasion to many censorious clerical gentleman for a pulpit wail about "the drama degenerating when actors stoop, by means of low and vulgar 'hits,' to cater to the vile tastes of the depraved habitués of the 'seventh heaven.'"

Among the "gods," besides the two classes of boys already alluded to, there are the urchin who, waiting at the door for every spectator to come out, asks, "Gi' us yer ticket, mister?" and the nimble little fellow who watches for a chance to get in, and finally slips in between ones lower extremities. Those who can "turn an honest penny" by running errands or following kindred occupations just long enough to "raise" the price of a gallery ticket, and those who hang around the theatre through the day and have a "hold" on one or more of the attaches of the house--the property man generally--for the performance of some trifling favor, find congenial company among the "gods" of the gallery.

This latter place is essentially the home of the "boys"; so much so, in fact, that the cunning youngster who slips through your understandings into the parquet will hasten to exit, and, with his check, hurry to gain admittance "upstairs," where he finds the company best suited to his tastes and habits.

Very many youngsters have no occupation and are therefore constantly out of money, but their love of drama-seeing is nevertheless ardent. And in order to procure a price of a ticket they go from door to door and beg pennies until they have the requisite amount. Most of them would not beg the price of their bread, yet they will go from house to house for hours to procure the price of the pasteboard which will admit them to the "god's heaven." This practice has been extensively indulged in during the present winter--the panic covering a multitude of mendicancies--by even full grown, young men, especially on the East Side.

There are those among the elder and more refined bunch of theatre-goers who claim for themselves the sole right to judge of the merits of a performance, and believe and repeatedly express the opinion that the deified juveniles of the "seventh heaven" are totally incapable of rendering an intelligent judgment on the merits or demerits of a performer. This is a mistake. A person may be refined in what is usually but erratically termed taste, and yet be unread and uneducated, and thereby as incompetent to judge of the literary quality and dramatic construction of a play as a newly arrived Chinaman.

Another person may have received even a classical education, but at the same time be as ignorant of what constitutes the perfect individualization of a character as an unborn babe; though such a person will rarely fail to put himself up for a competent critic, will recognize nothing dramatically intellectual outside of Shakespeare, and will bore you with the borrowed stereotyped opinion that "Shakespeare's vast, lurid and thrilling delineations of the strife of great passions never caters to the morbid taste of the low and vulgar." It is strange that this class of spectators never see vulgarity in the words of the Duke of Gloucester in Act I, scene iii--or in his and those of Lady Anne in Act II, scene i--and fail to notice anything immoral in the general tone and character of the play of "King Lear"; but mark how wide they open their eyes, how deeply they blush, and how loud are their cries at the obscene words of the woman who, in answer to the *roue* who accuses her of adultery, exclaims, "You were the first on my list, so help me God."

The "gods" find fault with neither. And sitting in their seats, and surrounded by the odor of tobacco juice and the sound of voices mingling oaths with laughter or applause, they render their unbiased judgment with far more discrimination than most of the spectators in "chairs" and "boxes" could do. With the "god," faults never pass unnoticed, nor is he miserly of approving plaudits in the case of meritorious art. Many a drama has been sent to the shelf by him and his friends. Many an actor, over-puffed and incapable, has been dubbed a "snoozer" and sent home with a flea in his ear after, at the longest, a week's "opening" eked out in the presence of empty benches. The case of less fortunate "impositions" has been settled at a first night.

The man endowed with taste will overlook a deficiency in the details if as a whole the performance is fair. But the "god" will lose no opportunity to express his dissatisfaction with any shortcomings of either the actor or the play. With him it must be perfection and no "between and betwixt" for compromise. No argument can be adduced to satisfy him that this or that is "good enough."

His manner of rendering judgment may not be so refined as that of the high priced spectator, but for that reason it is no less accurate. When he expresses his conclusion that such and such an actor "is a galoot," and that "the snoozer is a 'stick' and can't act worth a cent," in nine cases out of ten he is nearer to fact than the so called polished critic who informs you that the same actor "possesses talent which will eventually place him on the topmost round of the ladder of histrionic fame." And though the critic may not be a *stultus* in the sense of the "god," it is doubtful whether he is not at least biased, and whether, therefore, the adverse criticism, though roughly expressed, should not be accepted as the correct one. "Let justice be done, though the heavens fall."

[*New York Clipper*, April 11, 1874]

AN EAST SIDE THEATRE
by "Arab"

The Theatre. What recollections does the name conjure up! Recollections of some of the brightest lights that ever adorned our stage--Hamblin, Booth, Uncle John Scott, and all the others that played within its time-honored walls. Alas! many of them now sleep the sleep that knows no waking, and their places are but unworthily filled at present.

As we propose to visit every part of the house, let us begin at the bottom and work our way up. Here we are, then, in the pit, the "newsboys paradise." These enthusiastic patrons of the drama will often go without dinner and supper in order to save a shilling which will buy a pit ticket. The pit audience is usually made up of boys from the ages of seven to eighteen years, with a slight sprinkling of men. An artist would take much in interest in studying the variety of costumes worn by these boys. There is an argument going on a short distance from us between two promising specimens of young America. One has one boot and one shoe on and the other has a small sized flag of truce floating proudly behind him. The subject under discussion is the respective merits of Edwin Forrest and J. H. Allen as tragedians. The young gentleman with the boot and shoe is Allen's champion, while the flag of truce aristocrat does battle in behalf of Forrest. These are no oyster house critics; their minds are not prejudiced on either side by reason of their having partaken of champagne suppers. No, they give their opinions honestly and candidly; and if their language is not elegant, it, at least, has the merit of being very forceful. The dispute waxes louder and louder and the disputants are carried away by their subject. At last, Allen's champion, reduced almost to despair, rouses himself, and makes one last grand effort. "Forrest may be a good actor, but he can't begin to play "The Gunmaker of Moscow" like Allen."

Forrest's man is evidently staggered. He passes his hand through his hair several times, seemingly in search of an idea--or something else; but yet he speaks not. At this point of the discourse, another youth, with a hat that apparently belonged to his grandfather, and whose hands are "many a time and oft" employed on exploring expeditions over his cuticle, chimes in with a remark that, "Eddy is a d----d sight better than either Forrest or Allen."

Now, Forrest's man, having recovered from his former defeat, mutters something about Allen playing "Hamlet" at Pittsburgh. This adds fresh fuel to the flame. The debaters again resume their war of words. A resort to blows seems certain and a triangular fight--*à la* Peter Simple--inevitable. At this juncture a boy in front cries out, "Here comes Jack!"

And a new personage appears upon the scene, at whose approach every voice is hushed. The "autocrat of the pit." No monarch ever exercised more absolute power than does Jack. Tall and Herculean in form, few of the frequenters of this locality care to face him when he is in anger. The boys sometimes, when wearied with the toils and troubles of the day, extend themselves along the benches and try to woo "Tired Nature's sweet restorer." At such times, Jack, with quiet, noiseless step, steals behind the sleeper and, gently raising his coattails, deals him a gentle love tap with his rattan; and as the sleeper starts up suddenly with a sharp cry of pain, Jack allows a sarcastic smile to illume his somber visage but for a single instant; and playfully remarking, "You felt that, didn't you," stalks off in triumph.

The lights flash up and the orchestra take their places. They are welcomed with a yell; yet it seems but the ghost of the yell that used to welcome them in former times. At last the curtain rises and the boys greet the entrance of their favorites with various degrees of pleasure. At present, the heavy villain of the establishment bears off the palm in noisy welcome. The curtain falls on the first act and there is a general rush to the pit bar for refreshments. Beer is the usual drink and pig's feet the edibles most called for. Peanuts were once in great demand, but now they are apparently at a discount. Perhaps their popularity declined with the accession of the new generation of pit boys.

As we leave the pit we find a man standing at the door ready to pounce on one of his offspring who has visited the theatre against his wishes. Someone is likely to feel mingled pain and pleasure on this occasion. As soon as we regain the sidewalk we are surrounded by a crowd of boys, whose attire is in various stages of dilapidation and whose constant cry is, "Give us a check, mister?"

Suddenly the crowd scatter and the irrepressible Jack appears, while his blows fall thick and fast upon the culprits who, as soon as they reach a safe distance, make divers remarks derogatory to the personal appearance and character of the said Jack. All of which are received by that august individual with silent contempt.

We enter the first tier, and there we find a very mixed audience, working girls and their *beaux* predominate. One of the powers that be, with light overcoat and glazed cap perched on one side of his head, and swinging a little cane, patrols the passage at the back of the seats incessantly, big with the importance of his mighty trust.

It will be remarked that the girls often sit very close to the men, and that the latter, in many cases, have their arms around the girls' waists. Perhaps they place them there so that if the females should become excited by the acting they may be able to hold them in their places.

Here is a party of six, three pairs. Two couples are sitting close together in the manner we have before described. And of the third, the man is seemingly oblivious. He is lying on the seat, asleep, with his head pillowed on the girl's lap. One leg is thrown over the back of the seat; and by reason of his uneasy motions, he is in imminent danger of falling to the floor every instant.

Leaving the first, we ascend a flight of stairs and find ourselves in the second tier. Here the audience is mostly sailors. When a nautical drama is being performed, the criticisms upon the manner in which the principal character is being portrayed are not always very complimentary to the actor sustaining it.

Again we go up. We are now in the third tier. As we reach the top of the stairs, we find a woman and a man in close conversation. The woman's attire and bearing proclaim what she is. The man is said to be a detective. Perhaps the woman is betraying her lover to him, for her brows are knit and frequently a curse breaks from her lips.

We go into the tier and here we find a motley gathering of old and young gamblers, muscle men, fancy men, one minister of the Gospel, and prostitutes of all ages--from the girl of fifteen, just entering on a life of dissipation, to the woman of forty, who has been on the town for the past ten years. The language that is used in this place is spicy in the extreme.

Hark! A woman's scream is heard in the barroom and a general rush is made to learn the cause. We remain quiet and wait. Soon the crowd return to their seats and we inquire of a red shirted philosopher the cause of the disturbance. Slowly he drawls forth his answer, "Billy's woman called him a hard name and he mashed her in de bugle."

He seems to think beating a woman a matter of no consequence. The girl comes into the tier. One of her eyes is discolored and almost closed. In answer to a question from one of her sisters in misery, she replies, "I can't blame him. I called him a hard name and he split me."

That woman would sell the last thing she possessed in the world, perhaps even give the hard earned wages of her sin, to support that man. Yet, when in response to his ill usage she uses the only available weapon God has given her--her tongue--she is knocked down and beaten like a dog by him whom she would lay down her life to serve.

Let us take a look into the barroom. The walls are covered with crimson paper, and a number of cheap prints and miserable oil paintings hang upon the walls. A long bar extends along the front of the room and at one end there is what is called an "eating bar," on which, among other delicacies, are displayed the inevitable pig's feet. The bartender has no lack of custom. A girl is leaning against one end of the bar. A man enters and commences to talk to her. A girl appears at one of the doors and says, "Look out, Sallie, Jenny is going to tackle you."

"I don't care a d----n!" replies the girl at the bar.

At this moment, another girl, whose personal appearance is rather remarkable by reason of the extreme length of her nose, enters the barroom, her eyes flashing fire. She seizes the man by the arm and endeavors to drag him away from the girl at the bar.

"Jack, I don't want you to talk to that girl," says she.

"I'll talk to anyone I d----n please, Jenny," is the polite rejoinder.

Then Sallie makes a remark reflecting rather severely upon the chastity of Jenny; and in return for her kindness receives a blow in the face from the aforesaid Jenny. The bartender leaps over the bar and closes the doors; and the persons in the barroom gather round them to witness the fight. At it they go. Hats, dresses, feathers, flowers, and every other article of female apparel possible to destroy, are torn to pieces. Very few blows are struck on either side, the principal object of each seeming to be to inflict the most damage on the other's clothing.

After fighting in this manner a short time, Jenny cries out, "Sis, when you get enough, just holler."

"I'll never holler," replies Sallie.

And at it again they go, pell-mell. No blood flows; and the men, getting tired of looking on, separate them. And each of the combatants is surrounded by a little crowd of sympathizers.

There is another storm brewing and the doors are again closed; and another pair of pugilists step forth to do battle with each other. One is the girl with the black eye; the other is called White-headed Brad by the bystanders. Here is no tearing. The pair stand up and give and take like men. The "fair one with the flaxen locks" is soon vanquished; and the black-eyed heroine is borne off in triumph by her Billy, who has forgotten his anger in admiration of her fistic prowess.

Leaving this peaceful scene, we will go up higher yet. We are now in the gallery, "nigger heaven," as some call it. The smell of this place at any time is not quite as nice as otto of roses; and on summer nights it is most decidedly unpleasant to people with delicate olfactories. This is the place from whence oft issue cries of "Hoist the rag" and various other tokens of disapprobation when that portion of the "generous public," who occupy this part of the theatre, cannot command an unobstructed view of the stage. "Moke," "discounted nigger," and divers other complimentary names fly round thick as snowflakes on a winter's day. The remarks and criticisms on the performance here are in much the same style as those in the pit. Some of the contrabands who used to visit the old Broadway are loud in their denunciations of Manager Wheatley, because he does not give them a chance to see Ned Forrest and reserve a portion of the third tier at Niblo's for the use of "respec'able cullud pussons." The immortal pig's feet seem to be in as great demand in this portion of the theatre as any other.

Going down the gallery stairs, about every step of which has its own particular deposit of filth, we at last reach the street and once more breath pure air. This is no fancy sketch. The writer has not drawn on his imagination in a single instance. To everything herein narrated, he was an eye witness.

[*New York Clipper*, January 3, 1863]

THE BOWERY AND THE BOWERY BOY

The American historian who shall, in the year of grace 2000, essay to depict the customs and manners of his countrymen in the 19th century will, we deferentially infer, be somewhat puzzled to make a correct estimate of the influences of that Arcadian neighborhood yclept the Bowery. The times change. And it is fair to presume that one reason for the historian's dilemma will be the fact that the Bowery boy, who is now a flourishing institution, will then (alas! for the mutability of human affairs) be a thing of the past; and a correct estimate of his peculiar powers and abilities will then be an impossibility.

A Bowery boy can be likened to nothing but another Bowery boy. His manners and customs are erratic, and he has a complete conversational code of his own. He is much given to wearing the brim of his felt hat turned over the eyes (more over his eyes than on his head), to brushing the ends of his hair to the extreme point of his eyebrow, to clipping his words and running them into one another, to an enormous emission of tobacco juice, and to an extreme partiality for a "muss." His associates he generally addresses with "Say, Johnny!" and his whole bearing is a delicious admixture of easy familiarly, self-confidence and shrewd knowledge of the world.

If he should happen to quarrel with anyone, he has a fearful code of threats to which to resort for the purpose of impressing upon his adversary a wholesome fear of his own prowess before he comes to the ultimate arbitration of personal combat. Not the least of these is the threat to trample on that occult portion of human anatomy which is familiarly known in the vulgate of the Bowery as the gentleman's "puddings." So impressive is his manner of telling this that we run no danger of diminishing our self-respect when we confess that we had rather have the *cholera morbus* than submit to the indignity of having our "puddings stomped onto" by a Bowery boy.

But when he is at peace with himself and all the world, the Bowery boy is harmless enough. Not infrequently his opinions on current topics show a vast amount of shrewdness and wit; and his execution of a double shuffle in front of a hotel or Dutch grocery is impossible of emulation, except to those who are constant and loving patrons of the melodrama.

There is one good point about him, too, which is rarely found in his social superiors. He always sticks up for his own locality and its denizens. There is a story told on good authority, which says that two gentlemen from the Bowery one night visited the Italian Opera. During the performance, their conduct, although not at all noisy, was sufficiently marked to express the contempt with which their aesthetic taste condemned the entertainment. Coming away, one gentleman was overheard to ask the other what he thought of the "oppra." To which, quoth his companion, "Talk about yer Suseeneys and yer Brigneoleys and all yer other d----n furriners, why Teony Pester'd lick the skin o' the teeth off hafe a dozen of 'm."

Of the truth of which, in the peculiar line which Mr. Pastor has made his specialty, there can be no doubt. At all events, it is a sufficient criterion of the kind of amusement which the Bowery boy loves. The Bowery is nothing if not homogeneous, and the taste of one of its boys is equally the taste of all.

At night the Bowery is crowded with people of all kinds, pleasure seekers, fruit vendors, hawkers, apprentices, flashy looking and bejeweled gentlemen with very shiny hats and much cigar, work girls, and the *oi polloi* of the Bowery generally. There is plenty of laughing and chatting, not infrequently much practical joking, and a little quarreling. Some of the Bowery resort remain open late and do a flourishing business; and it is not till the early morning that the Bowery sinks for a short hour or two into the quiescence which intervenes between the business of one day and the next.

The streets in this part of the city are never thoroughly deserted. It is but a comparatively short interval between the teeming life of the evening and the opening of the stores in the morning. The dry goods clerk, who has seen vice defeated and virtue triumphant from the boxes of the theatre over night, takes down the shutters very early in the morning (his hair oiled and curled to the highest pitch of art, his appearance generally dapper and clean), prepared for another day's work, with intervals of surreptitious flirtation with the dainty young misses who take six-and-a-quarter gloves. If the inhabitants of the Bowery, then, are given to enjoying themselves after the devices of their own hearts in the evening, let it not be forgotten that they are among the hardest worked of the population during the day.

[*New York Clipper*, May 12, 1866]

PART IV: ABOUT PERFORMANCE

✿

TALENT AND TACT
HINTS TO A YOUNG PROFESSIONAL
by Bambrino

Some men are predestined from the cradle by their fond parents (*à la* Eugene Wrayburn and brothers) as to what their profession in after life shall be. But very few in such cases is the profession of an actor a chosen one; for even actors themselves, in some instances, are shy of recommending the dramatic profession to their children as a means of livelihood. Why? Well, there is an old proverb about treading on delicate ground and, theatrically speaking, the actor knows so well how proverbially "Fools rush in where angels fear to tread"; and there is another proverb, I believe, "The burnt child," etc. Again, the actor's love, ardent love, of his children is proverbial in at least the theatrical world. In a word, children of actors, when adopting the stage, usually do so from personal inclination.

Now it is a little singular to remark (and yet it is verified every day in conversing with actors) that many a predestined minister, doctor and lawyer ultimately becomes an actor. But it is not all singular, in any sense, that when a young man has tried his head and his hands at half a dozen pursuits (and all his own choice, for the ostensible purpose of gaining a livelihood and never gaining it) and has failed in them all, at some fated moment it should dawn upon him that he was born to ornament the dramatic stage. This interpretation of an unfitness for ordinary pursuits into a fitness for the stage occurs in some mind every day of every week in a year. And how amusing to note the consternation of the relatives (if non-theatrical) of the "ill-starred Tip" when he honors the profession and disgraces them by plunging into it.

...I once heard a clever actor say that any little knowledge of any trade or business that a man might pick up through his life [will] some day be of use to him on the stage; and since actors mold statues and shoe horses in the presence of delighted audiences, it seems as if he were right. But whether you have been of your own free will a rolling stone from one pursuit to another, or a predestined lawyer, preacher, physician--no matter what you have been heretofore--points but little in the aggregate as to your future success or failure on the stage. Having youth on your side and, we will presume, ordinary intelligence, if you have thoughtfully made up your mind to gain your living on the stage, stick to it through thick and thin, honestly persevere therein, learn the secret of patiently waiting for your laurels and patiently read the following hints, born of a life-long experience in theatrical matters. If you will act upon them and upon the greater incidental advice which the writer will quote for your benefit, you will do exactly what is calculated to make you a real actor in the best sense of the word.

At the outset of your theatrical career don't be over anxious on the subject of your talent. Young actors, as a rule, are an awful boor to themselves and others on that subject. "Do you think my talent lies in low comedy or tragedy?" "I have talent but who can show it in a part of two lengths?" "If I only had a proper field for my talents." And so they go on.

Now, what is this talent that there is so much talk about? Worcester defines talent as "a natural gift, faculty, ability." Ask nine actors out of ten (I should say young actors) if they think they have talent for the stage and they will undoubtedly tell you they have. Change the mode of interrogation and ask, "Have you a natural gift for the stage?" and five or six of the nine will doubtlessly hesitate to answer. Now, there is a much more encouraging definition of talent, and it is peculiarly applicable to stage talent. [It is] the definition of Galateo, who was born before Worcester or Walker or Webster was ever dreamt of. He defines talent as the "power of observation." Have you the power of observation? If you have not--and certainly it is not to be expected at your age that you can possess it in any great degree--you will have that power in the future if you keep your eyes and your ears well open. Cultivate this power of observation in the theatre, watch everything, hear everything, but say little. Reflect on what you see. Reflect on what you hear. You will be groping though, as it were, in the dark for a long time, but at last light will come.

As you cultivate this power of observation, perhaps, if your education has been neglected (and no blame, doubtless, attaches to you in that respect), you will soon discover--and the sooner the better for you in the end--that to achieve any position in the profession you must remedy that defect in some degree. If your social position has not heretofore thrown you into society where good breeding is cultivated, your power of observation, I hope, will (and perhaps painfully) awaken you to that fact. Strive to remedy that as well.

At the outset of your theatrical life you will probably fall into the usual error with regard to acting that most novices do, *viz.*, that acting can be taught. Let me assure you it cannot. Don't spend your money in paying masters of elocution. Stage business can only be learned by nightly experience and observation. Six months in a good theatre will teach you more than any actor living could teach you in years outside its walls. The lawyer, the physician and the aspirants of many professions have text books, lectures, instructors; but the actor who aspires to eminence and reaches it is self taught. There are guides to the stage which you will do well to read, but the instruction is necessarily limited. Those guides will all, however, impress upon you two things that are indispensable on the stage: learn to fence, learn to dance. Novices are proverbially awkward; and, failing to acquire those two accomplishments, they remain so.

It is somewhat amusing to see what delight a young actor feels when he first gets a long part to play. In his eyes, the length of a part makes it a good one. When young and inexperienced, don't mourn that you have so little to say in a scene. It gives you breathing time and time for that invaluable observation, which will ultimately do such great things for you.

In my schooldays I was taken to see "Donbey and Son" acted. The man who played Carker showed his teeth very much, and smiled and snarled at intervals, and must have acted the character to the life for it to live in my remembrance. This actor had not then gained a name of eminence and did not do so till many years after; but his power of observation was gradually developing. And when I saw Mr. Lawrence Barrett as Cassius at Booth's Theatre I saw what perseverance over many obstacles, among them being the disadvantage of personal appearance, had achieved.

But there are many men upon the stage, and who have been there for years, who never improve, who never rise beyond a certain point. This is owing mainly to the lack of the development of the power of observation and partly to the want of tact. Again, there are men on the stage of very moderate ability, lacking again the talent of

observation, but who rise in the business, star, and make a great deal of money. Shall I tell you why? Through tact. Again, there are men on the stage brim full of genuine talent, men who have studied hard, men who are ambitious and who would be favorites with the public had they always [had] favorable opportunities of exhibiting their talents to the public. But to this class the opportunity is wanting somehow for their talents to be judged. Why is this? Through lack of tact on their part. Now, you see, to succeed on the stage, though talent is essential in the main, tact has a great deal to do with. Tact is defined by Worcester as "skill, nice discernment," and by Galateo as "skill in using our talents."

I have shown you that men of ordinary ability rise in the profession through tact, and men of high ability often fail for want of tact. Now, with regard to the stage. What is this tact that you see is so eminently essential? It is what Lord Chesterfield vainly sought to teach his son and is sometimes called "a knowledge of the world"; and here you have the keynote to the success of some actors and the failure of others. It might amaze many an actor, while railing at his bad luck in the profession to the weary listeners of a green-room, if he were told that what he has said and done in the green-room and behind the scenes of the theatre has really been the true cause of his so called bad luck. Yet it is the case in many instances. Your knowledge of the world may be limited, but at least, as you know, the sober man has an infinite advantage over the man who is not sober; and, if in spite of that knowledge you drink through business hours, you will go down to ruin with your eyes open, with a legion of ruined actors vainly warning you back from that gulf.

Lord Chesterfield tells us that "books alone will never teach us the knowledge of the world,... but they will suggest many things to your observation which might otherwise escape you." I am very sure that if Lord Chesterfield had addressed his letters (in some instances) to actors instead of his son, they could not have been more applicable to them than they are. However, as very few people care to wade through his letters (though I should advise every young actor to do so), I will copy a few passages particularly adapted to a young actor's conduct towards a fellow actor,... with the hope that you will be sufficiently interested to search Chesterfield for yourself.

"There are no persons so insignificant and inconsiderable but may, some time or other, or in something or other, have it in their power to be of use to you, which they certainly will not if you have once shown them contempt. Wrongs are often forgiven, but contempt never is; our pride remembers it forever. Remember, therefore, most carefully to conceal your contempt, however just, whenever you would not make an implacable enemy. Men are much more unwilling to have their imperfections known than their crimes; and if you hint to a man that you think him silly, ignorant, or even ill-bred or awkward, he will hate you more and longer than if you tell him plainly that you think him a rogue.... We should never yield to that temptation, which to most young men is very strong, of exposing other people's weaknesses and infirmities, for the sake either of diverting the company or of showing our own superiority. We may, by that means, get the laugh on our side for the present; but we shall make enemies by it forever, and even those who laugh with us will, upon reflection, fear and despise us.... To know mankind well requires fully as much attention and application as to know books, and, it may be, more sagacity and discernment. I am at this time acquainted with many elderly people who have all passed their whole lives in the great world, but, with such levity and inattention that they know no more of it now than they did at fifteen.... Search, therefore, with the greatest care into the character of all those whom you converse with; endeavor to discover their predominant passions, their prevailing weakness, their vanities, their follies, and their humors, with all the right and wrong, wise and silly, springs of human actions which make such inconsistent and whimsical beings of us rational creatures...."

Never mind the croaker at your elbow who proclaims Chesterfield an "old fogy, out of fashion, obsolete." Doubtless, he would say the same of Shakespeare. Let no discouragement prevent you from adopting what your good sense tells you to be right. At another time I will show you how the power of observation may be cultivated in examples of living actresses and actors, and conclude with the saying, "We may give advice, but we cannot give conduct."

❦ ❦ ❦ ❦ ❦

That the theatrical profession is probably the most difficult one in the world to gain any eminence in, few will believe who have not been actively engaged in it. To the mass, the drama is but the pastime of the hour, and they can in no sense view it in a more serious light. Ask a printer if he does not now think he might have gone into a printing office the first day and have set up type as quickly and correctly, without the tedium of a long apprenticeship, and he will doubtlessly laugh in your face. Yet if a young man presents me with a ticket of admission to some amateur club to witness his first performance on the boards in the character of Richard III, I am expected not to laugh in his face, but to go and applaud and compliment him afterwards. And should I go, I would in all probability find his relatives--shrewd and sensible people, no doubt, in their own walk of life--assembled to witness my young friend make a fool of himself.

Nothing amazes and annoys regular members of the theatrical profession more than the frivolous and senseless way in which "outsiders"--educated people, too--view and speak of the player and his profession against the evidence of their own eyes and ears. These same people will pooh-pooh the idea that the committing of the words of a part to memory is but the least of the laborious tasks of a true actor. Tell them that it requires years of study to make an actor, and, though they may not laugh in your face, they will undoubtedly do so behind your back. Why? Well, we often hear people confess that they have "no taste for music," "don't know one tune from another," "no ear for it," and, by the way, if they said "no soul for it" they would be nearer the mark. But seldom, indeed, do we hear people confess that they have no taste for acting; for fifty men and women out of a hundred, if not openly expressing it, secretly cherish the belief that they are born actors and actresses, though they have no inclination to go on the stage. Yet of the fifty who shall go on the stage and fail, one half will never realize, wonderful to say, their own lack of ability or observation and their own personal disqualification for the boards as the cause. Actors and actresses know, if "outsiders" do not, that men and women, with rare exceptions, are not born actors and actresses, and become so simply through study, observation, and dear experience. Such as are termed born actors and actresses are persons with a naturally strong imitative faculty [but] who, in spite of brilliant prognostics, do not make brilliant debuts; for acting, after all, consists of something more than mimicry.

Now, the mischief arising from regarding the profession as one to which no apprenticeship is necessary, and as one that a person has but to walk onto to succeed and soon gain the topmost round, is not only detrimental to a novice but entails, besides, great loss of valuable time to him or her in correcting this false view. And many people are on the stage a long time before they get their eyes open to the fact that there is no royal road to acting; but that they must depend upon themselves, and through their own powers of observation be self-instructed, as has heretofore been described. When not acting yourself, go to the theatre and see others act; but you must not look at the performance with the same eyes as the man at your elbow. He comes for amusement; you come for instruction. He does not bother his brain how it is all done as long as he is entertained. You must see how it is done and not regard it as your entertainment. You will find it an irksome task but a valuable one.

The biographer of Master Betty (the once great prodigy) says: "Never having witnessed a performance before, fortunately his eyes first lighted on perfection," his first visit to the theatre being to witness a performance of the great Siddons. But one may learn a great deal from bad acting as well as good, for we may at least learn what to avoid.

If, for instance, in witnessing an amateur performance you will observe how these would-be players huddle together in a scene like frightened sheep, you will at least have learned to keep your distance from a fellow actor on the stage, I hope, if you would not yourself pass for an amateur. If you have ever had the pleasure of seeing either Miss Leclercq or Miss Fanny Davenport, or any other first-class actress in the character of Lady Gay Spanker, and should afterwards witness an amateur essay the same part, you will observe that the famous hunting speech, beginning, "There were sixty horses in the field," is entered upon by those ladies in a different way from the amateur actress, who will inevitably get up her steam immediately at very high pressure; and, consequently, not being able to increase in power and intensity as she progresses, her speech will fall flat and tame at the climax, and be rewarded by but a feeble round of applause. The real actress, you will call to mind, in reciting the famous speech, shrewdly rose, and by degrees of vigor, vivacity and vim, at the finale, brought down the house with well merited applause. This is technically called "working up a point;" but with observation you will soon discriminate in such matters for yourself, without any guide but your common sense and good judgment.

Let me give you one or two instances, however, of lack of observation in a real theatre, the drama being "The Sea of Ice." The mutineers tossed their muddy biscuits into the raging sea, said biscuits each falling with a crack on the boards behind the scenes, sending a general titter round the house; the Ogarita of the night dressed under the burning sun of the tropical country in the wrappings and skins better calculated for Alaska; the walking lady in a velvet train in a South American forest; and the Carlos of the night's costume embellished by a pink check shirt on shipboard; said Carlos, arriving in Mexico, having been shipwrecked, and finally coming into possession of untold gold and gorgeous Spanish apparel, when, lo and behold, he did not discard the pink-check shirt, but wore it still. Why dwell upon such trifles? Simply because these trifles marred, in a slight degree, a very fine performance, and to impress upon you that there is nothing on the stage, however trifling in the smallest detail, but is worthy of the attention of a true artist.

As there is light and shade in painting, so there is, or should be, in acting. The artist who ignores light and shade gives us but dreary pictures; and the actor (and he is of the type known as the "wooden" or the "cast iron") utterly dispensing with flexibility, which is the very essence of light and shade in acting, soon wearies his audience by his obtuse monotony. What ails the "cast iron" actor? Nature has not molded his features less facile than other men's, though we might deem it so to look upon his imperturbable countenance while on the stage; nor has nature set him apart, devoid of heart, soul and human sympathy. Oh, no! though to witness his acting one might almost believe nature had robbed him of every attribute except--well, say lungs and power of locomotion. Then, what ails the "cast iron" actor, whom no passion can rouse to aught save a senseless, ranting frenzy; whom no stage situation, however thrilling, however pathetic, however comical, can induce to yield a jot of his stolid manner; and whom no amount of stage experience, seemingly, can teach to unbend, though but ever so little, in his mockery of "holding the mirror up to nature?" Why, since he first put his foot upon the stage has he never once called his power of observation into play? That power, so to speak, is dead within him. What he had learned of his profession is the stage business in the humdrum of rehearsals. He has mastered the rough technicalities of stage business, and he has a good study probably ("cast iron" actors always have), and he can swallow thirty lengths and think nothing of it. He calls himself an actor, but he is simply a machine, who nightly grinds out the words set down for him, and mechanically goes through the routine of a performance as rehearsed, correct in entrances, exits, crosses, etc., and that is all; and herein he thinks his task accomplished. Talk to him of nature!--as well talk to the proscenium. He believes in "acting." Talk to him of embodying a character to the life!--as well talk to the moon and stars. Does he play a prince tonight, the next a pirate, you shall mark no difference but in the words put into his mouth and the dress on his back, and his voice will ever grate in the old monotony. His voice! He has trained it. It is the one thing needful on the stage. He is a master in elocution, and consequently never utters a word upon the stage in a natural tone. Dear young professional, avoid the "cast iron" school. Its followers never gain eminence or wealth, and are not in accord with audiences or with the higher grade of professionals.

Rossi, the Italian tragedian, gives an account of Miss Neilson, "your handsome English actress," coming to him for advice. She recited some passages from Juliet. And when she had finished he recited them after her.

She then said, "Mr. Rossi, if you are right, I am all wrong."

His answer was, "Miss Neilson, you declaim."

So, in playing a Shakespearean part, an actor or an actress may speak naturally without sacrilege. [When] uttering the words of the "divine William," one need not get on stilts to reach upward to him. He wrote for men and women, though often, to hear his lines spoken, you might not believe that general supposition. There is a saying, "The fool looking on is wiser than the man who is acting." So if any fool point out your errors in acting, take it in good part, whether so meant or not, and profit by it "though advice is seldom welcome, and those who want it the most always like it the least."

Remember that on the stage we are judged by what we do, not by what we can do. If you have talent, bide your time; it will be rewarded. Meanwhile, you need not entertain the green-room with your expectations or disappointments. There is nothing that a young man at his first appearance in the world has more reason to dread, and therefore should take more pains to avoid, than having any ridicule fixed on him. In the opinion of even the most rational men it will degrade him, and ruin him with the rest.

Many a man has been undone by acquiring a ridiculous nickname. Now, in the theatrical profession there is one especial nickname that you will do well not to incur, and that is "The Crushed Actor." If you feel yourself crushed and are discontented, keep the facts to yourself. You will gain no sympathy in publishing them, and may gain the above unenviable designation. Few actors are crushed but through some fault or folly of their own; and if you will calmly review your experience, you will see the truth of this.

Many young people about to go on the stage, ambitiously anxious to be doing, understudy (as it is called) a variety of long parts that they can have little hope of ever acting, [or] cannot act for a long time to come at least. This is not at all a good plan, for in such cases the student takes ample and leisure time to commit the parts to memory; and, as you begin, so you will go in the matter of studying for the stage. If you allow yourself ample time to learn a part, when actually called upon to study one at short notice, you will find it perplexing and difficult to do. To prepare yourself for such an exigency, commit to memory a part of say four or five lengths in a given time. Make up your mind to be perfect in that time; concentrate all your attention on the part. Meanwhile, think if nothing else. If you fail at first, still persevere, for you will have need in the future to congratulate yourself that you have done so.

Avoid the habit of copying out a part to assist you in studying it. This is needless labor and great waste of time. I have known actors, having once contracted this silly habit, who found it impossible afterwards to study any part without first writing it off; and many an actor having to study a character in haste is first at the necessity of first sitting up half the night (with the written part before him), setting it down in his own hand before committing a word of it to memory. Remember that the worst study will improve with practice, and those who have the quickest study on the stage soon forget a part and have shortly to restudy it again. Sit still while you study if possible. Pacing the floor while conning the words you will find exhausting and stupid work in the end. Learn your parts at home and not behind the scenes. No man can study properly there, and I never knew a true artist to attempt it except in case of emergency.

Nor does a true artist ever go upon the stage imperfect in the text except in a case of great emergency. A conscientious actor is always more or less nervous in a new part, to a certain degree even when dead-letter perfect; while, the "fishing for the lines" while acting makes a man or woman ten times as nervous. Ask any experienced actor if a man can play a part at all creditably who is imperfect in the words and his answer will be a decided negative. Actors all know there is no panacea in the world for stage fright. Being dead-letter perfect, plenty of rehearsals, taking plenty of time to dress, and using no stimulant to mitigate its horrors are the only known precautions available.

"Dutch courage," as it is termed, has, eventually, ruined more actors than dramatic incapability. And there is no more mournful sight than that of the poor actor whom habit has so far confirmed that he cannot face the footlights without a stiff drink, nor continue through the night's performance without a repetition of the dose between each act. All through your dramatic experience you will see that this treacherous aid finally defeats its purpose and leaves the victim a wreck in memory, intellect and reputation.

If you happen to be late for rehearsal, which you should never be, you need not kill off your wife's mother or some relative on that account, nor set your house on fire, nor set the hands of the clock back, for the lie will inevitably be discovered and you will share the notoriety on that score with a well known actor.

Gesture, grace and correctness upon the stage is highly important; but no rules can be laid down on paper that will be the slightest service to you in the theatre, though there are books written on the subject, and plentifully illustrated, which are highly amusing but not instructive. There are two people upon the stage, to whom it must be conceded, that are as near perfect in gesticulation as it is possible for an actor or actress to be--Mr. Lester Wallack and Mrs. John Drew of the Arch Street Theatre, Philadelphia. Either of these artists is a model in that particular for any young actor or actress. But few upon the stage, except those of a very high order of talent, define the difference in personating a villain between the gentleman and the boor. This remark is particularly applicable to the impersonators of the characters of Sir Francis Levison in "East Lynne" and the King of Spain in "Don Caesar de Bazan."

An endeavor has been made to show you that tact as well as talent is necessary to theatrical success; and what you do and say behind the scenes and in the green-room is quite as important as what you say and do upon the stage....

[*New York Clipper*, October 21, 28, 1876]

"INDISPOSITION" ON THE STAGE

We have frequently, within the past six months, been compelled to record the "indiscretions," to put it in a mild form, indulged in by performers on the public stage, not only in this city but in places where temptations are not so numerous. These "indiscretions," we are sorry to say, are not confined to the masculine gender, but included a number of the softer persuasion in the blacklist, and some of them, of both sexes, among the shining lights in the dramatic firmament. There are many actors in the dramatic profession who possess all the attributes of good performers, great histrionic powers, commanding presence, fine address and rich melodious voice, combined qualities that make up the excellence of the artist. If an actor abuses these gifts, he becomes not only the wreck of the man but of his genius.

We have all long since learned of the downfall of Addams, Ingersoll, Perry, Eaton and others, who at one time shone with luster in the dramatic world. If those who are now toiling through their theatrical apprenticeship, and to whom the stage is to look hereafter for its artists, are encouraged to emulate the sad example of those we have named by the supineness of our audiences, we can have but little hope for the future greatness of the histrionic profession.

Although instances are not uncommon of public performers appearing on the stage in a state of intoxication, yet the press is silent upon the subject and audiences appear indifferent. What if the great Kean, Cooke, Booth, Fennell, Webb, Addams, Perry and others exhibited their "eccentricities" upon the stage, and had their "indiscretions" glossed over by a forbearing public? Does it follow that the "eccentricities" of those men are to be emulated to insure success? Yet many assume this to be a necessity and essential to histrionic fame. The public should teach them the fallacy of such reason by hissing every "indisposed"--or intoxicated--performer off the boards.

Booth's "weakness" gave him the character of an eccentric man, and as this eccentricity tended to make him popular, others in the profession sought to imitate his weakness and his eccentricities in the hope of becoming equally popular; but they lacked the genius of the man they sought to imitate and they soon fell to rise no more.

In a number of cases brought to our immediate notice, "indiscretion" and "eccentricity" culminated in bestiality and a drunkard's grave. A popular actor of the day has so frequently appeared upon the

stage in a state of gross intoxication that many who go to see him perform do so for the purpose of witnessing some eccentricities not enumerated in the bill. Another has been tolerated so long that his drunken antics have become a part of his attractive powers. And yet another has been permitted to insult his audiences night after night by appearing before them looking more like a bummer than anything else; while his appearance on the street, occasionally with a pair of black eyes, has been the signal for mischievous urchins to cry out, "There goes the drunken actor!"

And we are very sorry to have to say that certain actresses here and in Europe are no better than the men in this respect. We have known instances where these "drunken ladies," as the children would call them, have been gallantly led off the stage by the actors; and their non-appearance for the balance of the evening [was] accounted for by the plea of "indisposed."

What performers do off the stage is not the business of the public, we are given to understand. But the public have a voice in the matter when these orgies are continued on the public stage, disgracing not only the actors but the noble profession of which they are unworthy members. The people who patronize our places of amusement should not permit these "eccentric" performers to come before them in a state of "semi-consciousness." The press should speak out boldly on this subject and decry a vice that seems to be increasing with such fearful rapidity. Let them condemn all performers who make a public display of their drunken gymnastics and it will not be long before the nuisance is abated.

The worthy members of the profession, who are placed in an awkward position by the "eccentricities" of those with whom they are compelled to associate on the stage, demand a reform in this matter. It is due to the public that they should no longer be insulted by the vulgar performances of drunken actors. The press and public can control this matter if they will. Let the good work commence at once.

[*New York Clipper*, December 28, 1867]

THE STAGE IN AMERICA
FROM AN ENGLISH POINT OF OBSERVATION
by Wardle Corbyn

To cross the Atlantic only a few years ago was a feat that created great dread and demanded much forethought and preparation. Now
it is so common that a day's notice, a wide-mouthed bag of necessaries,
and your ticket are all you require. Once on board a Cunarder or one of
the White Star floating palaces, you may, if a tolerable sailor, reckon
on nine or ten day's holiday, free from business, bustle or bother of any
kind. You breath the purest ozone, eat, drink, and make merry, read,
chat, gamble a little, go to bed early and get up when you please, make
pleasant acquaintances and sometimes friends, and in a week and a half
land in New York, the most cosmopolitan city in the world. Theatrical
artists in great numbers cross the Atlantic constantly, by far the greater
number going westward; as scarcely any but stars come from the States,
while stock and star, operatic, dramatic and terpsichorean find a wider
field, better remuneration, and much less competition in the United
States than in Europe.

. In all the chief cities of the thirty-three states which form the
American confederacy there are fine, spacious theatres, many of which
are elegantly and luxuriously embellished and liberally supported. In so
brief an article as this it would be impossible to give even the slightest
account of these. I shall, therefore, only describe a few of the theatrical
features of New York, as compared with those of London.

The latter city, with a population of three million, has thirty-
eight theatres. New York, with about a million people, has fourteen....
It is also certain that in America star actors and actresses are richer than
in any other part of the world. Edwin Forrest is rated at a million and a
half dollars, say £300,000; Charlotte Cushman, £70,000; John Owens,
£80,000; Barney Williams, £50,000; Joseph Jefferson, £60,000; and,
with the exception of Mr. Forrest, all these fortunes have been gained
in the last twenty-five years. And I recall many happy days passed with
the other artists when they were one and all "stock." It is evident that,
to those stars who hit the popular taste and become favorites, the United
States is an El Dorado, and wealth flows in upon them in a golden
stream.

To the "stock" actor or actress in England who thinks of visit-
ing the States, I would say, "Unless engaged for a permanency with an

American manager, STAY AT HOME." The pernicious system of engaging artists "by the job"--i.e., for a week or two or for that very indefinite term, "the run of the piece"--is, I regret to say, even more prevalent in America than here; and under that system I have seen really competent and popular performers acting in three different theatres in three consecutive weeks, or traveling from city to city every week or two to fill a part in the cast of some star's play. Besides, "stock" actors and actresses of undoubted ability and experience are plentiful in America; and the managers can find easily all the artists they require.

Mediocrity is at a greater discount in the States than in England. The Americans are lavish in their payments for first-class talent, and no country in the world has rewarded great artists so liberally as they have such celebrities as Jenny Lind, Fanny Ellsler, Sontag, Grisi and Nilsson; but second-rate artists are silently but certainly suffered to sink.

Our cousins are quite as demonstrative as we are in applause; and in that modern innovation of floral offerings they beat us out of the field (or garden) by presenting their favorites with gigantic baskets and pyramids of flowers, or harps, ships, temples and monograms, formed of wickerwork, concealed by lilies, pinks, roses and camellias. But these costly and really beautiful *cadeaux* are not flung or pitched onto the stage, as with us, but gracefully handed from a proscenium box or carried round by the ushers to the stage door and exhibited on the stage when the act drop or curtain is raised to a "call."

On the other hand, Americans seldom hiss [and] never at a lady. They quietly leave the theatre and religiously keep away from it while the objectionable piece or person remains on the bills. *En passant*, I heard a hiss converted into a hearty round of applause one night in a New York theatre. An unfortunate "utility man" had a line to utter which unexpectedly offended one of the audience, and he hissed--a loud, clear, traveling sibillation. "Utility" paused, looked straight at the spot whence the sound appeared to come, then stepped forward and said, "Only two things in nature hiss, the goose and the serpent--which are you?" A hearty roar followed, and no more hissing.

The New York theatres twenty-five years ago were the Park, the Bowery, the National, the Chatham, and Palmo's Opera House, the first home of the lyric drama in the United States, which of course ruined its projector and enriched scores of artists and laid the foundation of the love of Italian music, and has led to the erection of a half a dozen at least of magnificent opera houses in that country.

Then, the Park Theatre was the central and most fashionable theatre in the city, and Niblo's, nearly a mile above it, was considered too far up town. Now the Park, the National and the Chatham have disappeared and Niblo's is literally lower down town than any other. Above Niblo's in Broadway, or branching off east and west, we now find the Olympic, the Globe, Wallack's, the Union Square Theatre, the Academy of Music, Fechter's, the Fifth Avenue, Booth's, the Grand Opera, the St. James', and Wood's, not to mention a dozen variety shows, minstrel halls, &c., in the great thoroughfare, and the Bowery and Stadt Theatre on the east side of the city.

The American theatres generally are built on a larger scale and much more luxuriously fitted up and furnished than those in England. The Academy of Music, Booth's Theatre, and the Grand Opera in New York are really magnificent buildings; and in all of them the comfort of the audience is provided for in the most liberal and perfect manner. Niblo's, which has just been re-erected, is described as one of the most admirably constructed theatres in the world.

One striking feature to an Englishman, and most satisfactory, is the actual, not imaginary, absence of all "harpy" extortions. No "fees" are either demanded or accepted for booking seats or sitting in them after you have paid extra to secure them. Programs are handed freely to all visitors. A courteous and silent usher conducts you to your seat and retires. No bawling of numbers or banging of doors, which are quite as unnecessary in a theatre as in a church. Another custom claims attention, and, I think, approbation. No matter how great a number of people may assemble at the boxoffice in the morning to secure seats in advance, for that or any other evening, no person attempts to pass or stand before anyone who arrived before him; but falls into his place and forms one of a single file and quietly awaits his turn, as do those behind him.

The tickets are supplied much more rapidly than when half a dozen applicants are struggling and clamoring for them at the same time; and as there are really no "fees for booking" to pay, the transfer is rapidly effected. It may appear incredible to an English playgoer, accustomed, *nolens volens*, to the rough and often dangerous "rush" on the opening of our theatre doors when any great attraction is announced; but it is a fact that when a star or a piece draws thousands to a theatre in

New York, the same quiet, orderly and agreeable system is voluntarily adopted and carried out by the audience themselves, at night as well as by day. Those who have secured seats beforehand pass quietly to their places; and each gentleman who desires to purchase tickets takes his turn, and his ladies await him in perfect security in the lobby.

Another noticeable feature in New York theatricals is the custom, almost universal, of commencing the performance at eight o'clock and finishing the whole entertainment at half past ten or, at the least, eleven o'clock. This plan enables people to dine leisurely and be in their seats as the curtain rises. It spares the actors the annoyance of playing a *lever de rideau* to half empty benches, bawling ushers, and the banging of box doors and the equally painful process of "playing out" the *exigeant* few who remain after the principal piece is over.

The audience, being seated from the commencement, you are spared the intolerable nuisance of late comers passing in front of you to their seats, interrupting your interest in the performance and destroying your peace of mind generally. You sit out, without fatigue or *ennui*, the whole entertainment, refresh or sup at your leisure, and reach home at a reasonable hour. The adoption of this system at our London theatres would save the manager's pocket in gas, give the artist and employees shorter hours, and enable them and over 20,000 people who visit our theatres nightly to devote an hour to supper or lighter refreshments, and allow them, as well as the tired publicans and outside sinners, to retire at midnight.

[*New York Clipper*, December 30, 1876]

ON STAGE MANAGEMENT

Audiences, when they watch a dramatic performance, have, ordinarily, a very vague idea as to the means by which the result before them is attained. They know in a sort of indistinct fashion that an immense array of people is required, and that scene painters, costumers, mechanics are among the most indispensable parts of the staff of a theatre. But further their knowledge does not extend. Those who are in reality and in all senses behind the scenes become the possessors of knowledge which not only alters their opinions as to the value or significance of certain representations, but considerably modifies their views on acting in general. A dramatic representation is obviously not a melee, a scrimmage in which everyone takes what place suits him best, in which the strong take the best places and the weak go to the wall. No doubt the strong, theatrically speaking, do triumph over the weak and usurp all the best places on the stage. But every position and attitude seen upon the stage is arranged beforehand, and by incessant rehearsals every actor on the stage becomes acquainted with the routine of his own business and the position he is called upon to occupy.

Discipline stricter than that enforced upon the stage is scarcely enforced in a regiment. The necessity for the observance of discipline is, of course, patent to every observer. None will question the all importance of system, and all will readily believe that such remarkable effects as are at times produced can only be accomplished by the subordination of all the occupants of the stage to the volition of one mind. When the stage is converted to an exquisitely arranged *parterre*, one knows at once that every place is fixed beforehand. And when the radiantly clad ballet opens into the likeness of a blossom, or folds into that of a bud, it is obvious that every motion is arranged beforehand with minute and scrupulous attention. But what is not generally known is that the same care which arranges the position of each nymph of the ballet extends to that of hero and heroine, of gruff father, or of comic footman. No action of any of these, in ordinary cases, is the entire product of his own individuality.

Over all reigns one will, that of a mysterious being known as the stage manager. The public sees the name of this functionary in the bills, and does not trouble itself much to guess what may be the nature of the duties he is called upon to perform. Amateur actors have an idea that the power to which they have been compelled to yield a turbulent submission is real, but to others the term "stage manager" conveys no idea whatever. Yet the stage manager is the real despot of the stage, against whose fiat there is, in the majority of cases, neither rebellion nor appeal. His importance can hardly, in any sense, be overestimated. It is scarcely too much to say that the choice of a stage manager is almost as important a matter as the choice of a company. Where the acting at a theatre is good, sharp, and distinct, where the parts all seem to fit each other, and the business of the stage is always quick and effective, the stage manager knows his business. When he is weak, unskillful, or slovenly, the stage speedily shows it. Order no longer reigns, the acting becomes slovenly and ineffective, and all goes as badly as it may.

It is thus seen that the acting, at any epoch, depends, to a limited extent, upon the stage managership. A stage manager, it is true, cannot give soul to an actor who has none, but he can make the most possible of a stick, or he can very effectually repress and discourage the talent of a clever young aspirant. In judging of the merit of an actor it is almost impossible always to make the allowances which are necessary to do him justice. He may himself be equally conscious with the critic of the defects and inelegancies of his own representation, and yet find himself as powerless to remove them as any one of his audience. Over him stands the stage manager, whose judgment is final, and who, in support of his own opinion, is obstinate as a rock. Many a time when the audience marvels at the stupidity of an actor, who in spite of criticism persists in doing something altogether preposterous, and concerning the propriety of which no two opinions can exist, he is, in fact, blameless. An actor persists in wearing his hat in a drawing room while talking to a lady, sits down and crosses his legs while she is standing, or walks up and down the stage without any reason whatever. Wherefore? An incompetent or possibly malevolent stage manager has directed such proceedings; and the actor, however indignant he may feel, has no remedy left but to obey and to face the obloquy he had not deserved. Where actors are young, this tyranny is very keenly felt. An older actor learns how to keep the letter of the command and break somewhat of its spirit. Obey he must, but he will manage to obey as little as possible.

On the stage, as in all other cases, moreover, the great fishes break through the net wherein the smaller fishes are caught. An actor or actress who has made a thoroughly high position becomes, of course, the master of the stage manager, who has to defer to his judgment. All this is done according to his or her wishes. The stage is grouped so that the remaining figures may furnish a background as effective as possible to the figure of the star. The front and center of the stage are his by prescriptive right, and all the acting manager has to do, if the star is not himself acting manager, is to dispose of the other characters that they are all subordinate to the star, and in no manner whatever interfere with his movements. But the hardship presses the more grievously upon the tyro, because the star is exempt. It renders the difference between them more great and conspicuous. Many an actor has ground his teeth with anger and annoyance at finding himself charged with stupidity and incompleteness for actions the absurdity of which he saw while he was compelled to perform them.

Stage management is, however, a most indispensable thing in a theatre, and, in pointing out that it becomes in individual cases a hardship, we are not attempting to deny its general utility. Nothing is plainer than that someone must exercise command in a theatre, and that he must have power to enforce obedience which will only be grudgingly yielded. Where, as on the stage, everybody desires to excel, and everybody has a notion that he has the capacity to do so, the results without some form of despotic government would be hopeless anarchy. A stage manager is, therefore, in fact, a necessity.

Nor is his office without great advantages. At least as much is done by a stage manager for an actor as against him. If the tyro is frequently compelled to do foolish things, the folly of which he sees, he is at least as often prevented from doing absurd things he would have otherwise attempted; or instructed to adopt good positions and attitudes on which of himself he would never have hit. Indeed, the extent to which well known and even famous actors have been indebted to stage managership would never be surmised, and will not readily be believed. Many of those attitudes, starts, and other devices which have most arrested the attention of the audience, and have been accepted as strongest proof of an actor's genius, are due to the talent of the stage manager.

A stage manager watches carefully and knowingly the motions of an actor, sees an awkwardness, and suggests some movement the effect of which is magical. How important, then, is stage managership we have shown. That it is liable to abuses is undoubted, and that it may be an instrument of repression undeniable. Its effects, however, are, on the whole, beneficial rather than injurious to the majority of actors; and whatever injury it may at times inflict upon an individual, it more than compensates for [it] by the benefits it confers upon his fellows.

[*New York Clipper*, June 15, 1867]

THE DRAMA
by "a retired actor"

The world has been well compared to a stage and man is a poor player who, if he acts well his part, is sure of a rare benefit when the curtain falls upon the last act of the mysterious drama of Life, enacted within the great theatre of Time. On the other hand, to transpose the foregoing, all the stage is a world and all the players merely men and women, as will be clearly seen by this our hasty peep behind the scenes.

The drama is the great art of arts, at once the most vivid, the grandest, the most beautiful and perfect of all, as it is "The art divine, in which the sister arts their charms entwine." Many of the masterpieces of literature have been presented to the world in the form of drama; both genius and piety in all ages and countries have been supporters of the stage--in some instances writing for it, in others acting upon it, and in some both writing and acting, as did Shakespeare.

The profession of an actor is at once ancient, honorable and arduous--as difficult of access, whithal, as it is to abandon after one has once fairly "rubbed his back against the scenes," as it unfits one for aught else, and there is attached to it a strong and peculiar charm which nothing else can supply. It is the player's office "to hold the mirror up to nature," "to catch the manners living as they rise," and thus, as says the great "bard, who fore ran the ages," to form "the abstract and brief chronicle of the time." The qualifications requisite to constitute a good actor are varied and manifold, as there should be united in his mind and person a rare combination of gifts and graces, among which a good voice, face and figure--in form, power, gracefulness and expression--a fine memory, self-reliance, etc.; and he should also be proficient in the arts of singing, dancing, fencing, dressing and making up. He should likewise possess a good education, being especially familiar with history, should be a close student of human nature, and above all should be possessed of that exquisitely susceptible temperament which is an inseparable and indispensable characteristic of the true artist. Even though lacking some of the above-mentioned qualifications, one may nonetheless become a good, nay, even a great actor, as Garrick, Cooke and Booth (the physically small), and the elder Kean (with a vile voice), who upon the proud pinions of their peerless genius soared beyond the very clouds. Success upon the stage depends largely upon the selection of the line of business, that for which one is best adapted being determined by experience only, for it is frequently the case that while the taste lies in one direction the talent lies in another entirely opposite, as in the case of many famous comedians who at the beginning of their dramatic career aspired but to the higher walks of tragedy, and many eminent tragedians who fancied themselves fit only for the very lowest of low comedy.

The author of this little sketch for a long time fondly aspired to and foolishly imagined that he would shine, nay, fairly blaze in theatrical glory as Macbeth, Othello, Richard III, etc; but at length, after many bitter mortifications, he became known only as a very "eccentric old man." Yet let the afflicted be consoled, for verily it takes the wisest man to play the fool, just as a humorist in literature must ever be the deepest thinker; for, in order to joke well on any given subject, a most profound knowledge of the subject in question is ever an invariable prerequisite.

The comedian is generally the most serious and intellectual of the entire company. Good ones are rarer than good tragedians, as in the world we ever find too many to make us weep, but too few to make us laugh. The tear is ever ready to flow at the merest trifle, carelessly uttered by a mere child or even an idiot, while to evoke a smile often requires the highest powers of genius. The clown in his motley garb, the comedian with his painted face, the humorist with his goose quill are among the greatest benefactors of mankind, for the great mission of mirth is to cheer and strengthen, to purify and refine, to expand, elevate and ennoble the human soul. Often, however, when the most amusing to others, he is himself the saddest of mortals; as for instance in the case of the great and inimitable Liston, viz.: one of the most eminent medical men of that day in London, whenever medicine failed to operate favorably upon his patients, often gave his final and, as he declared, greatest prescription in the form of these simple words: "Go and see Liston!" till at length one day the most woebegone of all human beings presented himself to the doctor for examination, who told him that he only had a fit of the blues, and that the best thing that he could do would be to "go and see Liston."

"Give me a mirror then," responded the poor sufferer, in accents the most melancholy.

"For what?" said the doctor.

"Because," quoth the unlucky wight with a visage of despair and in a most sepulchral voice, "God help me, I am Liston."

An actor has many masters to please, among whom are the public, the press, company, manager, author and, most difficult of all, [the] conscientious artist himself; and all this, too, when the play is printed one way, cut in another, rehearsed in another, and performed in another. Or he may be ill, have a poor part, be cast out of his line of business, or be obliged to take a part at short notice, or those having scenes with him may be imperfect and ruin his best points; nevertheless, of all this the public takes no note, but judges him simply by the effects which he produces.

Perhaps the best time to study is at night, though not too long at a time or one, instead of learning, unlearns. By study, the memory becomes wonderfully developed, so that some are able to wing their parts, though a quick study is attended by a forgetfulness as speedy, and vice versa. At times, without any apparent cause, memory suddenly and momentarily forsakes even the oldest actors, the mind becoming but a perfect blank; and that, too, in some part which he has played many times, and which he knows backward as it were, or like the very letters of the alphabet.

In all well regulated theatres there is, of course, a prompter, though sometimes he fails in the performance of his duties, and there are many old actors who are unable to take the word from even the best prompter. It is an easy matter, comparatively speaking, to memorize a thing to be recited to a few friends in a quiet room, though a decidedly different affair to learn that which is to be declaimed amid noise, bustle, hurry, sudden changes, the strongest glare of light, before strangers, for money, and that too in an artistic manner. Again, it is difficult to study a skeleton part from a manuscript, when one knows but little or nothing of the story or the relation of his own part thereto, and has nothing but cues to go by, which too often are not given. Actors have a saying that "good parts make good actors," and another that some parts are so good and fat that they play themselves; nevertheless, a true artist will do his best to improve a poor part in the playing, while by his careful performance of a good part he will try to render it even better....

The oldest actors are at times very nervous when playing a part for the first time, when with a new company, or before a strange audience; and, indeed, I never knew a good performer who was an exception to the rule. The advice of the great Booth (the elder) to a novice who asked him how one could become a good actor was to "be natural," and that embraces the thing in a nutshell. Forget yourself and

all the rest will come; lose yourself in your impersonation, forget your own identity, and the presence of the audience, and you will act well in your part. This is, perhaps, the most difficult of all to accomplish, and only genuine talent, united to a sufficient amount of experience, can enable one to attain this great end.

An actor is obliged to rely wholly upon himself. By his own merits must he rise, as by his shortcomings must he fall. Nor can he employ a substitute, nor defer the performance of his duties; but upon the arrival of the hour, like a soldier, [he] must be at his post, prepared to discharge his duties promptly and to the best of his ability. Alas! too often the tinkling of the little bell, which is the signal for the rising of the curtain, though so musical to the ears of the expectant audience, is to the luckless performer like the great knoll of doom. Little does the public dream of that which an actor suffers when not up in or shaky in his part, or when playing with a new company, or before a strange audience, though he tries to console himself as best he may with the poor player's proverb: "Twelve o'clock will come."

There are those, I regret to say, who, being alike destitute of respect for themselves, the author, manager, company, audience, and their noble profession, constantly neglect the study of that which is assigned them, being able, as they style it, to "fake" through even the longest representation, or to cackle an endless number of lengths, which they substitute for the text of the author. Thus, while the audience pay for one thing they receive another, a fraud as shameless as it would be for a grocer to furnish a customer with sand instead of sugar or with sawdust in place of meal. This is also called "fluting" or "gagging" through a part, [which] in the best theatres is heavily fined as the serious offense that it is. One law at least should be most rigidly enforced in every theatre in the universe, and that is the one so clearly laid down by Shakespeare, who wrote from the most ample experience as an actor, viz.: "Let your clowns speak no more than is laid down for them."

There are two branches of our subject which are great arts in themselves, that of dressing and that of making up. One with a scanty wardrobe, with proper taste and knowledge, can make a better appearance than one with an extensive wardrobe who knows little or nothing of costuming. And one who is proficient in make-up can thereby, in a measure, atone for many deficiencies while he heightens the effects of his other merits.

I have frequently been unable to distinguish at first sight actors, with whom I was playing, when a short distance behind the scenes--once mistaking my old and highly esteemed friend, the late sterling comedian, William S. Forrest, who, refined gentleman as he was, I imagined to be some old vagabond who had stolen into the back door of the theatre. Upon a certain occasion, while playing at the Providence Academy of Music, my own uncle, who had known me from babyhood, and who visited the theatre for the expressed purpose of seeing me perform, utterly failed to recognize me even though favored with a front seat in the parquet and though I was on and off the stage nearly the whole time. Thus, too often, when a young man while playing old men, many people positively declared that, far from being young, I was really but the "lean and slippered pantaloon" which I represented. True, in addition to an elaborate make-up, I filled out the picture by an entire change of voice, walk, gestures and manner.

Though the temptations are many, actors are but seldom guilty of grave offenses. Their virtues are great, their vices of the minor order, and of the members of no other profession, not excepting even those of the clerical, can one say as much. Their toil is unremitting and severe, their recompense but small. Their expenses are heavy, yet they are by all odds the most generous people in the world. Their politeness is proverbial. With their study of and insight into human nature and character, their taste for the artistic, whether humorous or pathetic, their talent for recitation and mimicry, their musical abilities, and their minds so fully stocked with the choicest gems of literature, it is no wonder that their society is sought by the most talented members of all the other professions. And can we not have charity for their little weaknesses when we consider their late hours, peculiar temptations, and the great and constant strain upon nerve and brain, in their efforts to console, amuse and instruct their fellow man? Often, too, are they obliged to study and perform when they are in the greatest agony of body and mind; and yet bravely do they conceal their pain and grief, presenting us with the smiling face, before which our own sorrows are splendidly dissipated.

Inspiration will do much to sustain the powers of the true artist. And I have known many cases where actors were taken from beds of sickness, borne in a carriage to the theatre, dressed and made up by their brother actors, laid upon couches in the wings, raised and support for their entrances; yet when their cue was given they made their entrance upon the stage and played their scene to perfection, though at their exit they sank down exhausted--and so on from scene to scene, till at length the curtain went down on the last act, when they were taken back to their sick-rooms, weaker than ever, the public being utterly unconscious of the double part thus played by the suffering performer, or of this real tragedy enacted within the mimic tragedy, or perhaps comedy.

In that beautiful poem, which has been designated as the most perfect specimen of verse in the English language, "An Elegy in a Country Churchyard," Gray says, with equal truth, force and beauty:

> Full many a flower is born to blush unseen,
> And waste its sweetness on the desert air.

Thus, while there are actors occupying positions which they are incompetent to fill, on the other hand there are those who circumstances have kept with the brilliant light of their genius obscured and hidden behind the clouds. The greatest tragedian as well as the greatest comedian I ever saw (both, alas! now dead) were but members of strolling companies; so that they were often supported by mere sticks, and "threw their pearls before swine," as it were, as but few of their country audience could appreciate even a hundredth part of their transcendent genius. The greatest "eccentric old man" I ever saw--in fact, a genius of the very highest order--I encountered years ago in an obscure village on the western frontier. Through my advice he went to New York, obtained an engagement, became an immense favorite, starred through the principal cities of the country and Europe with the greatest success, and is now the possessor of a princely fortune.

As we have said, an actor is often called upon to study a part at short notice and without sufficient time for preparation. Many years ago, as I was sauntering leisurely along the streets of the city where I was then playing, enjoying the sunny afternoon, contented and happy (for I was smoking a superior cigar, and was up in my little part of old Tobias in "The Stranger"), my joy was suddenly transformed to sorrow, and in fact I was cast upon a bed of the sharpest thorns by the merciless manager, who pounced upon me at the street corner with the request that I would study old Solomon to play the same night, as the first old man of the theatre was seriously ill and unable to perform. As there was no remedy for it, and it was "just to oblige, you know," off I posted to my hotel, studying like a race horse till the time to go to the theatre, when I played the dreaded part and by good fortune made a hit.

Another time I was called upon at equally short notice to study Polonius in "Hamlet," one of the longest and certainly the most difficult to study and play of all the old gentlemen of the drama. From the moment I began to study the part until the performance of the same was fairly concluded, I suffered torture. I could eat nothing whatever, which was a great help to me, as the mind (and voice) was thereby in a better condition than it otherwise would have been. In short, I went to the theatre as a lamb went to the slaughter and as the butcher goes to the lamb, expecting to both murder and be murdered--to murder the part in the first instance, and to be murdered for my pains by the audience. I trembled so violently that I could scarcely dress or make up, responded to the interrogatories of my brother actors incoherently and like the very lunatic which for the time being I really was; and yet, strange to say, was afterwards "cool as a cucumber," dead-letter perfect, even prompting the others on the stage with me, and at the close of the performance was complimented by all in the highest manner for my original, excellent and perfect conception and rendition of the quaint old father of the mad Ophelia. Nevertheless, when Hamlet was supposed to stab me behind the arras, my dying groans were, to me at least, sounds of the highest delight, after the last of which I danced a most inimitable jig solo with the greatest gusto imaginable. Since that well remembered time I have played many long and difficult parts, but never have I finished the performance with such a sense of relief, joy and pride as I experienced upon that ever memorable night when my lips gave such a joyful utterance to the expiring groans of the murdered (by Hamlet) old Polonius.

[*New York Clipper*, June 15, 1867]

PART V: ABOUT THEATRICAL PROMOTION

❃

ON BUSINESS MANAGEMENT
by Dramaticus

The business manager is a very important personage in the administration of the theatre. His position corresponds to that of the stage manager, who reigns abaft the curtain, while the business manager controls the front of the house--the manager being presumably the power behind the throne. Inasmuch as there is a business manager attached to every theatre, there are a great many of them, but few really good ones. He may be ornamental as well as useful. He is the secretary of state, through whom all the negotiations of the little world are transacted. To be a good business manager, that is, one who, besides faithfully discharging his duties, is a credit to the establishment he represents, requires the suavity and finesse of a diplomat, and the incite into character of a prefect of police; for his duties bring him into contact with all classes, and he can just as well as not make friends with all, if he has the tact.

One of the most important duties of the business manager is that of "attending to the press," as the phrase is; for there is much that he delegates to the treasurer and stage manager. Now the critics of the various papers are as different in personal peculiarities as the journals they represent. Some are young men with the follies of their age; some are middle aged with wills of their own; a few are old men with antiquated ideas. Some are to be flattered by attentions and insidious laudation; some are to be converted by arguments and explanations; others are to be let merely alone until they come round of their own accord; others are glad to be assisted by suggestions and hints, which they in their ignorance thankfully receive; while another would very properly indignantly rebuke the business manager for presuming to dictate to him. Others (I fancy I hear some parasite of the press adding to himself) "others are to be paid." Well, I'll take him at his word and suppose that some such as he are to be paid; if not, the thought is the son of the wish. But there are black sheep in every fold, and these are soon known; and I am not in the least afraid that these fellows will ever be mistaken for the gentlemen of the press who are not paid.

It is true--to continue this digression--that the critics are often blamed for articles that appear in the column they are supposed to control, which are inserted by the proprietors and publishers thereof (the higher power) in return for extra advertising or contracts for illustrations. But even these, I am happy to say, are exceptional cases. Attending to the press, therefore, requires great delicacy and taste. Little Flibbertiggibbetty, who imagines that everything he writes is of the greatest importance, can be easily wound round the managerial finger, figuratively speaking, by flattery and attention. I have known a simple regret, that his article was not suitable for quotation in the circular for provincial enlightenment, to cause him to write one (a puff) that would be. He imagines he is very important, and that is why his articles are reproduced by the managers.

It is needless to say that such a course would not answer with Philomet, who is a thoughtful, able writer, with the modesty that frequently characterizes merit. He would indignantly repel such familiarity. He is too old a bird to be caught by chaff. His obligation to his readers is greater than his vanity. The peculiarities of each critic has to be studied. This one is sure to lose his temper unless he is sent end seats; while that one wants a private place to himself in which to write his article, which the manager will send down for him to the paper for the next morning. It is needless to say that the gentlemanly and educated business manager has a great advantage over his less urbane and enlightened brother, in that his society is congenial to the critics, as that of any well informed man would be. Between this class and the critics there often springs up a friendship which the others cannot understand, and naturally attribute to wrong motives.

Another embarrassing duty of the business manager is often delegated; this is locating billboards and conciliating those on whose premises they are placed. And this involves also delicate transactions with rival bill posters and, often too, rival printers; and by an ill considered word or hasty action in dealing with these people the theatre may be compromised more than is apparent. It is the prime duty of the business manager to work up all outside matters conducive to the popularity of the theatre.

The duties of the business manager are more varied and not so stereotyped as those of the stage manager. He is manager in the absence of the manager. Although he has important duties to perform, he is something of a figure head, and is often put forward as such. For instance, when the great unknown (and often unwashed) genius presents himself at the box office window with a manuscript roll under his arm, he is referred to the business manager, who treats him according to the mood he is in at the time. To him is sent the ambitious aspirant after Thespian honors, whom he also angles as the whim takes him. It is amusing sometimes to see the business manager thus play the autocrat. With this little brief authority, however, he can blight the hopes of struggling genius.

He has his foibles like all of us, and is often governed by them. The foibles and idiosyncrasies manifest themselves in various ways. It is certainly a foible when one of them would claim mention in all the notices of his theatre for doing nothing more than the duties for which the manager engaged and reasonably pays him. There are some business managers who are so clever in the art of cajolery that, in chatting about everything but their theatres, they provoke the critics to solicit information thereof; and then impart the same to them in a manner to place the recipient under obligations to them.

It is generally the business manager who writes the programs and advertisements in the theatre (In circuses there is employed, to do this and pertinent work, an "editor of publications" or "director of printing."). The advertisements are often characteristic of the style of the man. As there is everything in the way in which a star or performance is billed and advertised, much depends on the ability of the business manager in this direction. There was a time in this city when a certain prominent and talented actress' name could not be mentioned without eliciting the exclamation: "Clutched the dramatic diadem at a single bound," which was then the prominent line in the announcements of her engagements.

Alliterative headings and lines are studied by many business managers. The writing of playbills and posters is an art. It is not so easy as one might suppose to make the announcements satisfactorily in few words, so that each may be prominent. The object is to have the announcement in large letters, so that he who runs may read. Authors should bear this in mind in selecting titles. Robertson evidently was actuated by this principle in selecting his monosyllabic titles. Some of the

"The Great Society Sensation"

DIVORCE

titles of the old comedies are long enough to run around a corner. The business manager and the star often squabble about the announcements.

The genus of business manager may be divided into three classes: the gentlemanly business manager, the boorish business manager, and the conventional business manager; all of whom have in general the same duties to perform, yet discharge them as differently as the distinction implied by their classification. Though, after what I have said, individualization is not necessary.

The gentlemanly business manager endeavors to make it pleasant for all who have intercourse with him, and so he wins many friends. Having friends among the members of the press, his theatre generally receives many notices, to the disgust and bewilderment of the boorish business manager, in whom no one takes any interest, and who assures every critic that his neighbor has been bought over by his rival, and that there is a conspiracy formed against him. I have called him the boorish business manager for want of a better word; but I cannot find one as expressive, for he is a bore, with his conspiracies and insinuations.

This is an age of enterprise, change, novelty; and the conventional business manager, like the traditional stage manager, is passing away. He has well nigh outlived his time. He cannot adopt the new phrases employed in contemporaneous announcements. He lets rising talent slip from him and make the fortune of other establishments, because he is not wide awake enough to know that, to have achieved their provincial name, these youngsters must have improved since he saw them years ago playing utility. I call him conventional because he simply performs his obvious duty; there is no tradition to guide him as [with] his friend, the veteran stage manager.

I might tell of one of my friends, who is always so solicitous for a personal notice; but, as it would in a measure be betraying his confidence, I won't. I will say, however, that I returned him his elaborate manuscript puff of himself one day, with regrets that I could not publish it.

One business manager does not favor any more than a simple announcement on posters, giving the space to the cut, which can be taken in at a glance and the story understood at once. Another evidently has a great horror of those fearful and wonderful cuts (As Charles Reade, whom I see in *London Society* particularly requests that his story of "A Simpleton" shall not be illustrated, which is, I suppose, the reason why the *Harpers* have given no pictures of Poyn and the

Doctor), and indulges in highly ornate letters. I must say that, except for sensational blood and thunder, these fancy lettered posters are preferable, as no wood cut can do justice to a nice comedy set or a spectacular display.

One business manager has a theory on the subject of crowded houses, and no matter how long or short, or, in fact, whatever the article may be on his theatre, he is contented if the statement is made of crowded houses. Another blandly declares that the "press can accelerate success or failure, but can produce neither;" but always endeavors to get puffs I notice. From the business manager who is always talking about his business, reiterating and expirating and complaining, like a fourth-rate Methodist extorter, without the sense to make himself interesting and to see that he is a boring one, heaven save us!

[*New York Clipper*, December 14, 1872]

ADVERTISING AMUSEMENTS

Under despotic forms of government the tradition is enforced that "His Royal Nibbs," the King, holds his power by divine right. It is a pleasant fiction, about on a par with the absurd notion which obtains in this country to the effect that all our people are sovereigns, when in a point of fact many of them are scoundrels and some of them are scavengers. But whatever may be said of the divine right of kings or the sovereignty of the people, it is certain that the claim to royalty in the show business rests on the basis of printers' ink. The Prince of Showmen was not born to the purple. He established his title and built his palace and filled his exchequer and secured his retainers, all by means of judicious advertising.

The generous public kindly permits the giver of amusements to estimate his own worth and position; and if he but estimate them highly enough, they usually concur in his verdict. We speak no parables. The greatest showman is the showman who makes the greatest announcements, who advertises the most; for it follows as a natural sequence that if he advertise much he must have much to advertise. Few men are such fools that they will deliberately invite attention to that which is not worth seeing; but many possessing that which is worth seeing fail to invite attention to it by adequate advertising.

We suppose Jenny Lind was a great singer. It would be treason to the memories which haunt the minds of all who saw her on her first appearance at Castle Garden to say that she was not the Queen of the Lyric Stage. It is well nigh a quarter of a century ago that her grand debut was made in this city. Advertising was in its infancy. Singing was the uncertain expedient whereby doubtful artists gained a precarious livelihood. High prices for anything in the line of amusements were unknown. And yet, Jenny Lind sang to a sixteen thousand dollar house, to more money than was ever paid before or since for a single performance in this country or Europe. The tickets were sold at auction. The man who paid the highest price was a hat and fur dealer. He did it as an advertisement, and, considering the trade which it brought him, it was a very good investment. We recall an epigram written at the time which sums up his case:

> Don't think there was any revealing
> Of a heart which could easily melt;
> It was not a matter of feeling,
> But simply a matter of felt.

The whole triumph of Jenny Lind was the legitimate fruit of advertising. Unquestionably, she was a good singer; but of all the multitudes who attended her concerts, not more than one in a hundred had heard her name before her advent to these shores. If she had appeared unheralded, unadvertised, she would have sung to empty benches. If she had been moderately advertised, she would have achieved moderate success. She was overwhelmingly advertised and, therefore, her triumph was overwhelming. It was a simple sum in progression which Mr. Barnum solved to his own profit and satisfaction.

We do not wish to be understood as intimating that the mere spreading of printer's ink is a passport to success in the management of amusements. Advertising is a fine art. Mike Walsh used to say that it required more education to cross Broadway in a crowd than to teach school in the country; and it certainly requires more genius to advertise a show properly than to do either of the other things.

No rules can be laid down for the guidance of advertisers; but the effect of all good advertising is to excite the reader's wonder and pique his curiosity. A mistaken notion prevails in some quarters that unpronounceable, polysyllabic nomenclature--big words coined from doubtful Greek roots with bastard Latin terminations--may be usefully employed in advertising. We think that idea has been carried too far already. The best advertiser is not he who airs his own learning most, but he who arrests the reader's attention by a direct appeal to the reader's taste or fancy. For instance, thirty-six years ago the gentleman who is now the greatest merchant in the world, Mr. A. T. Stewart of this city-- captivated half the trading population by the simple announcement he was "selling out at cost." The phrase has been worn so threadbare in latter years that it is no longer available. It has done such extensive service that the children of this generation can hardly believe that it was ever new. But its use by Mr. Stewart was wholly original. It was during the panic of 1837 that he started the novel advertisement. He actually sold goods at their original cost; but he was enabled to buy them much below cost from the merchants who had failed or were failing.

These cases of Messrs. P. T. Barnum and A. T. Stewart illustrate boldness and skill in advertising. They are selected because each was the first of its kind, and because each led the way to great achievements. Showmen will hardly fail to appreciate the lesson they teach. Bold advertisers must have something worth advertising or no continued success will follow their efforts. A show possessing no merit whatsoever will draw a large house "for one night only," if it be skillfully advertised; but the man who thus gulls the public would best keep shady for all subsequent time.

It is nearly a dozen years since a bogus wizard filled the papers with announcements of a performance which he was to give at the old Academy of Music. It was just after Hermann had completed his first successful season of prestidigitation. This pretender beat Hermann in advertising. He completely captivated the public by his amazing promises. Finally the evening of the performance dawned, and the Academy was crowded with a brilliant audience who had purchased tickets at a high price. What followed is well remembered by showmen in this city, and it is a tradition among the profession everywhere. The bungler was hissed from the stage; but he cleared a thousand dollars by the operation, and fairly illustrated what might be called the "brute strength" of advertising.

The successful and judicious advertiser will never yield a point to a competitor. If he finds that it requires a full page of a newspaper to set forth the merits of a rival concern, he will also have his full page, and will endeavor to make it bristle with sharper points and abound in warmer adjectives. Nor will he be content to rest on his laurels at any time. No matter how large his business, how flattering his prospects may be, he will continue to advertise as if he had just embarked in a new venture and had still a name to make. Any letting up on the part of the manager in this particular is construed by the public as a sign that business is falling off and that he has found it necessary to curtail expenses.

The *Clipper*, in offering these hints and suggestions in regard to advertising, is governed by no selfish motive. We are abundantly satisfied with the advertising favors showered upon us by our innumerable patrons. But an experience extending over a score of years has taught us that the value to showmen of advertising liberally can hardly be overestimated. Many an entertainment of real excellence, which languishes now for want of support, could be pushed into paying prosperity by the free use of printers' ink. No manager can afford to forget that the Prince of Showmen is the Prince of Advertisers.

[*New York Clipper*, June 14, 1873]

THEATRICAL MANAGERS AND THE PRESS

The most ardent admirer of the stage cannot deny but that during the last half century there has occurred a gradual, yet most effectual, decline as to the general appreciation of dramatic performances. Not that the patronage bestowed upon places of public amusement has in the least degree decreased; for, on the contrary, there are few branches in trade which have proven more lucrative to both performers and managers than the theatrical profession. Nevertheless, however satisfactory the pecuniary results may chance to prove to the followers of Thespis, we are forced to admit that the stage, as a civilizing institution, has almost imperceptibly forfeited that standard of dignity, that omnipotent influence upon society, it was wont to possess in days long since gone by.

A hundred reasons have been alleged to account for this untoward mishap, each one of which may have contributed, either directly or indirectly, to the general result, inasmuch as a permanent effect is only to be accomplished through a multiplicity of causes. Yet with these it is not our province to inter-meddle at the present moment, as we treat the drama with respect to the condition in which we find it,

irrespective of retrospective prejudices. Nevertheless, there are abuses palpable to the critical eye existing in our present dramatic system, which if not eradicated threaten to reduce the standard of theatrical performances to a still lower level than that to which they have up to this time descended.

We do not complain of the paucity of acting ability at this moment distinguishing our metropolitan stage, when contrasted with the exuberance in talent overflowing the theatres a few years back, inasmuch as it is beyond the power of mortal man to controvert the economical principles regulating the condition of supply and demand. Neither do we find fault with the deteriorated literary qualities of the plays now in popular vogue; for, if the critical sensibilities of the audience be not vexed by the incongruities in language and plot, and their extravagances are tolerated through a craving for novelty and scenic effects, it is simply evidence of that very deterioration in taste to which we have already alluded.

But there exists a gross abuse connected with our theatrical managements, alike unjust and injurious to the audience and those beneath managerial supervision. We allude to the sycophantic adulation extorted from the press by influential managers, who, through forestalling criticism, deceive an audience as to the merits of a piece or of the performers in it. It is this playing upon the venality of journalists, this destroying the reliability of sound, rational criticism, which, in our judgment, has contributed to the decadence of the drama, in our metropolis especially.

To exemplify the practical workings of this prevalent system, let us instance a case far from imaginary. A manager, investing heavily in a speculation founded generally upon some novel triviality, considers the subornation of professional critics a portion of his duties. To this end he devotes a portion of his capital, as a business item, to secure a certain space in journals possessing large circulations, or having a reputation as reliable guides in such matters. Employing the services of a competent writer, sometimes drawn from an influential daily, in the hope of propitiating his good grace, but more frequently maintained as a stipendiary to his own establishment, the manager crowds the newspaper columns with adulatory comments upon the enterprise in which he has embarked, which, prepared at his suggestion and beneath his supervision, present a rose colored and generally delusive view of the character and merits of the performance in which he is personally and pecuniarily interested. The public at large, ignorant of the source whence the articles emanated or the motive of their dictation, naturally rely upon the reputation of the newspaper for critical sagacity and honesty in opinion, and become, as it were, entrapped into pre-judgments on the merits of the piece; for none can deny the fact that there exists a potency in the expression of opinion by even the most obscure of journalists which tempers his reader's frame of mind and exerts an influence over his immature judgment, swaying it by involuntary prejudice.

Such a condition of affairs could not have existed during the palmy days of the drama for two cardinal reasons. In the first place, there would be difficulty in discovering an editor or responsible manager of a journal so oblivious to his personal dignity or to his sense of public duty as to loan himself to the publication of that which, at the best, would be but an *exparte* statement of presumptive facts, provided he was aware of the design and intention of its composition. Again, the theatrical critic of those days, being generally a gentleman of erudition and of reputation in the world of letters, would consider his prerogative invaded and his reputation endangered by an anticipation from another source of the judgment the public naturally expected to come from him in a frank, honest and independent exposition of professional opinion. But nowadays, we are sorry to say, theatrical criticisms, which are and ever should be reliable items of information, falsification of which is as disgraceful as perversion of patent facts, are regarded by a number of journals as mere advertising notices, whose fallacy is extenuated upon the ground of pecuniary compensation in common with other announcements of the business world.

In fact, metropolitan managers have introduced into this country the Parisian *claque* in its most obnoxious form. Not content with cramming their houses with "dead heads" tutored to the art of applause, whose boisterous demonstrations are misinterpreted as the spontaneous expression of the auditor's opinion, resort is had to an imposition of stipendiary criticism upon the general public, purporting to come from an unbiased sentiment of journalists, the integrity and reliability of whose judgment on all matters of popular interest we are inclined to accept as that of experts in their particular line of business. In this way ruling the public press, or a portion of it, whose necessities and avarice have placed them at the knees of the coin-dispensing potentate, the manager is enabled as well to foist fraudulent wares upon the public as to tyrannize over the dependents of his company.

We cannot overestimate the evil effects of this pernicious and degrading system upon the dramatic profession. Were free and unbiased criticism to be allowed as in days gone by, when such men as Washington Irving and Paulding contributed seasonable and healthy critiques to the daily and periodical press, the public would look to the journalists, as they then did, as safe guardians; while actors would peruse critical comments to glean information, and for the correction of their errors. By our managerial bridling of the press, neither of these objects, the cardinal aims of pure criticism, can, by the remotest possibility, be attained.

The deceit of the public may be extenuated as a trick of the trade, but nothing can be urged in palliation of the injury inflicted upon the profession, who, to subserve managerial purposes, are suffered to persevere in a course of erroneous acting until habituated to a vicious style in declamation and manner, which could have been averted at the outstart through the exercise of critical judgment. There are dozens of so called stars, bepuffed and bepraised by the press at managerial suggestion, utterly deficient in the rudiments of their art; and who, had their errors and shortcomings been judiciously pointed out by competent critics, and the hints acted upon by artists, would have rendered themselves competent and conspicuous members of their profession. On the other hand, there are scores of obscure actors and actresses assiduously trained to their calling, wasting an existence which would prove honorable to the stage were they not perpetually hidden beneath the bushel of managerial interference, which apparently values merit proportionally to the noise it can make in the newspaper world.

We have called attention to the existence of this managerial evil in the hope of its abatement through the resumption of independence by our journalists, hitherto loaning themselves as accomplices to a premeditated fraud perpetrated upon a community who will not fail to reprove, in course of time, the mercenary insincerity of those in whom they have placed reliance. We are aware that it is useless to appeal to managers for any alteration, however just, in their established habits; and therefore, in exposing a piece of duplicity, we charge it upon those who, if they be not the real authors of the scheme, are consenting parties to its accomplishment.

[*New York Clipper*, September 19, 1868]

THE
RED
LIGHT

THE STAR SYSTEM

A fruitful cause of complaint among theatrical managers is the large sums demanded by popular actors for their services. The star system, as it has come to be known, is emphatically condemned and its effects are held to be wholly injurious to the stage. The matter is one which calls for honest discussion. Much sound argument can be adduced in favor of the manager's side of this question. The rates demanded by the popular star appear exorbitant when measured by the pecuniary reward which offers itself to other kinds of labor, either physical or mental. The star shines only upon condition that he shall receive a large sum as a certainty or a heavy percentage on the receipts. The manager who is compelled to pay sixty cents of every dollar taken at the boxoffice to a single performer naturally feels that he has cause to grumble. With but two-fifths of the receipts, he is left to meet all the expenses. Such a seemingly unfair division of the profits necessitates economy in other directions; and so the company engaged to support the star is too often of inferior quality. The performance is strong only in the head, lamentably weak in all other parts. And even with this enforced economy, the manager finds that his margin of profit is discouragingly small.

Take a successful metropolitan theatre as an illustration. Suppose the receipts of seven performances aggregate five thousand dollars. The star takes fifty percent (Some take even more), which leaves the manager twenty-five hundred dollars. From this the salaries of the stock company and the numerous attaches of the house, with all the expenses of rent, advertising, lights, and incidentals are to be deducted. The surplus, if there be any, is left for the manager. And that is all. But, apart from the question of profits, it is urged that the star system injures the stage from an artistic point of view: that the absorption of so large a proportion of the receipts by a single actor tends to lower the standard of the performance as a whole; that it discourages the members of the stock companies; prejudices the manager against experimenting with any new play which may possess acknowledged merit, but which is without the prestige of popularity; removes stage representation from the realm of true art and makes it simply the framework for the display of individual talent. It is the star, and not the play, which people go to see. All this may be asserted, as indeed it frequently is, by the opponents of the star system. But then the star has something to say on the other side of the question.

Assuming the star is really an artist and that his ability is conceded, upon what basis shall an estimate be made upon the true value of his services? The manager's prompt response will be: "His power to draw." The critic might say: "His power to act." Our supposition is the star should meet both requirements. He is able to act and able to draw. What are his services worth, he asks? Is it too much when he demands half of the receipts? Consider that question in its pecuniary bearings first. Without the star the performance would attract but few. There would be no receipts to divide. If, then, the one performer is able to fill the treasurer's box, where without him it would be almost empty, may not this one performer in justice demand a third, a half, or even two-thirds of the receipts? So argues the star. The manager complains because his profits are small; yet, without the star, there could be no profits whatever.

Consider the question next in its bearing to art. Why, somebody asks, should one actor receive more for a week's work than many of his profession earn in a year? The answer to that natural inquiry involves more than can be embraced in this desultory discussion. The surgeon performs an operation which requires half an hour, and sends in a bill for a thousand dollars. He earns his money with wondrous ease; but it has taken him a lifetime to fit himself for that half hour's operation. Tennyson is paid more for a stanza than the newspaper rhymester could obtain for a canto. Twelve square inches of canvas, with the touch of a master's brush upon it, sells for more than a panorama. The reporter does three times as much work as the editor-in-chief, and he gets one-tenth of the latter's pay. It is not for the mere reading of the lines that the star demands a larger sum than is paid to all the company combined. He asks to be rewarded for the years of training, for the study and tireless effort, which alone have fitted him for the position he occupies. Nor should his success tend to discourage, but rather to stimulate, his fellow actors. He shows what it is possible to achieve; it is for them to imitate him if they can.

[New York Clipper, December 1, 1877]

PART VI: ABOUT THE MUSICAL STAGE, ETC.

NOTES OF A LEADER OF ORCHESTRA
by Charles Connolly

There are but few lines of professional business that catch more sarcasm and funny comment than the serio-comic branch. The criticisms concerning the serio-comic's voice, dress, morals and chronic chaos in the matter of husbands seem to be in everybody's mouth. But it must not be forgotten that in the present state of break-neck acts, rib-crackings falls, broadly farcical sketches, and sensational acts of every description, the lot of the single young party who follows any of the above noisy specialties, and essays to please an excited audience with a round of songs, is decidedly not a happy one; while, as to the matter of husbands, it must occur to even the most prejudiced mind that these things do occasionally occur in private life among some of the gentler sex who are not serio-comics to any particular degree. Fair play is a--chestnut.

The juvenile lady, who, after knocking us all speechless with the broadest kind of an unnecessary "father," petulantly asked what sort of a hotel the manager was going "to chuck us into next," deserves our warmest thanks for "bringing us to" so immediately (if abruptly), even though we felt alive in the ear-tingle for many weeks after whenever the distressing solecism would return to us.

Smiggles, king comique, after years of theatrical and vocal work, surprised us all by buying a country residence, which he calls Smiggles' Willa. The willa cost him between $200 and $2,000. After a long spell of drinking, he went out and got sober one day, lost his head, and "gave away" the surprisingly agreeable fact that he paid for it in installments and had nineteen years in which to pay off the above mysterious sum. This struck us all as a nice, easy way to buy a willa.

Whenever you hear of any professional buying anything like that, it sounds harder to do. Here is Smiggles with his willa and nineteen years to pay it in, while the rest of us are dependent upon the good nature of our landladies. However, he knows it's all right, but desires that the details be not given away lest the paralyzing effect of the purchase be destroyed; so we simply but fearlessly state as a matter of incontrovertible news to professionals generally that Smiggles, king comique, has really purchased a country residence and that the same will be generally known as Smiggles' Willa if you please, and thanks.

A certain comedian asserts that he can cause the cornet player in the orchestra to balk and blow out false notes by simply catching his eye while he is playing the sketch music, and then taking out a lemon and sucking it. He claims that the sight will make the unfortunate cornettist's sympathetic mouth pucker to such an extent that the reliability of his lip will be destroyed to the consequent temporary destruction of his embouchure.

"The Mascotte," with chorus and orchestra, was lately played at a Western dime museum. How have the mighty, etc.! The street pictorial display mixed up the opera crew and the museum curiosities in startling contrast, and the characters were pasted in and among Indians and buffalo things without the slightest regard to the blend. At another museum a couple of swell song-and-dance artists gave the manager two years' notice on discovering that they were billed under the two-headed calf. It would be an exhilarating sight if the lecturer, after dilating on the beauties and attractions of the curiosities, should in a moment of forgetfulness stroll into the theatre portion and proceed to expatiate on the distinctive peculiarities and incomprehensible habits of a few of the performers.

"What makes them always get so mad at the end?" was the thoughtful question once put to me by a very young, but very precocious miss, referring to the usual musical racket and physical commotion which seems to be indispensable to the proper finish of orchestral overtures. A quaint and natural observation, to be sure, though not so completely cheering as the story of the young miss who, after listening to a beautiful vocal trill, told the lady "how nice she gargled!" As discouraging to the lady, this was, no doubt, as it is to the violinist who, after months and months and months of practice to master the peculiar arpeggio bowing on the four strings, is requested to please do that funny wiggle with the bow again!

The viola is the modest little instrument in the orchestra whose deep tones and round filling-up of chords aid so much to give strength and beauty to the accompaniments. The viola is typical of a class of people in this world--though a very small class--who do their work in a solid and effective manner without ever attracting any special attention beyond the knowing few, while the bass drum will probably suggest a much larger class, who, with nothing but wind and noise to recommend them, are continually intruding themselves and their work on everybody's attention, and who won't be ignored. The viola is very often missing in song arrangements for small orchestras; firstly, because a great many cheap arrangers fail to "pick up" a knowledge of writing for the clef of this instrument, and secondly because it would possibly cost the cheap performer just ten cents more.

Did you ever think over the talk in a green-room, and try to imagine the cause of such a wide difference of opinion in a circle that naturally should tend to one center? If you were to talk to each one separately you would find that all would agree, or nearly so, on a subject that, when brought up by general conversation, would separate them almost as entirely as if they were different nationalities.

I recollect giving an entertainment with a concert party in a room used for the storage of carriages. It was a fearful night, and one would hardly think that a sufficient number of people could be brought together to be entertained. We employed the drayman to take us to the hall (it was impossible to walk, so we thought), where we found an audience of a hundred people eagerly awaiting the arrival of the "show folks." I think seven feet would have covered the distance between floor and ceiling, and no sign of lath or plaster greeted the eye of the party-- in fact, nothing but a goodly number of joists, which supported the floor above, and a post scattered here and there, dimly visible from the light sundry candles gave forth. Immediately after our arrival, a gentleman came in with a lantern, when some one of the audience suggested that the candles be put out, and the lantern used as a chandelier. It created a general laugh, which showed us at once that the people had come to enjoy themselves and would be well content with what we could do, in spite of the surroundings.

Previously to this, each member of the company had been grumbling about the place, and what they could not do. Now it was different, and all went at their several specialties with a will and made up an entertainment so far ahead of their expectation that at the conclusion they were wishing for such a place to play in every night. Had it not been for that opportune remark, we should have gone home and given up the night's work and the money we could ill afford to lose.

If we would try more generally to work together, and not think of what we can not do, we would soon note a wide difference in the cashbox, and also note again, in an artistic sense, that is almost wholly lost sight of in the indulgence of some imaginary nothing. Particularly is this applicable to beginners. When you attempt a new act or part, do it with a will; give no thought to the surroundings, but recollect that your audience are your judges and not your companions.

I know of no other business that is so fraught with jealousies as ours; and if in a measure they could be done away with, it would be a stepping stone in the advancement of our largely increasing profession. It does you no good to dishearten or cry down another, but rather makes an enemy of one upon whom, at some future time, you might be glad to call for assistance. A pleasant word or a kindly act is never out of place, and you have a lighter heart for giving it, even should it never be returned. You sing with telling effect such songs as "Never push a man when he's going down the hill," but as soon as the "wing" covers you, you push the one who, at another time, may be able to give you a helping hand. Try it when opportunity offers, and, mark my word for it, you will note the effect, and agreeably, in a much shorter time than you had anticipated.

Years ago the attempt was made to elevate the tone of a theatre in one of our western cities, and for that purpose a fine stock company had been engaged, composed principally of New York actors. Well, it opened, but did not hold out, and one of the managers was firm in the belief that a Jonah was at the bottom of it. The straws drawn, it fell to the lot of one who was really the most talented member of the organization, and in fact a growing favorite. Every conceivable annoyance was brought to bear so successfully that the party was forced to send in his resignation, which was accepted at once, and for the time every one was satisfied (in imagination). But business did not come up as anticipated, the project was abandoned, and the theatre fell back to its old grade and unflourishing business. Now, the reason was simply this--the class of people who were in the habit of attending that place could not appreciate real talent, or, if they could, were not willing to support it. I don't think there are half a dozen actors in the United States who have seen so few of the downs as that Jonah, if I except the one that used to sing "Maggie dear," and went home from Syracuse through the good will of the company, who were stuck there.

Breaking a looking-glass is another hobby. A leader who now stands high on the star list once told me a mournful story of a company to which she belonged, and after a tearful recital concluded by telling me that they broke a looking-glass the first day they started on the road. Another instance, that I was interested in myself, and over which I have often laughed, is this: I was standing by an open window in my dressing room one night, when a white pigeon, lured by the light, flew in upon my bosom. I took it immediately to the green room to show the ladies, when, to my surprise, I was the recipient of more commiseration than I thought was my due. My pigeon was not complimented as I had supposed it would be, and through the thin partition I heard such remarks as, "I would not have had that happen to me for anything in the world," and "There's going to be a death in the company, I know." No one died and no bad luck befell the company, which made a pleasant trip to St. Paul and return, arriving home with well-filled coffers.

A scenic artist, who now resides in Suckerdom, gave me his opinion of Jonahs as follows: "I came down to my room one morning very early to fill in some ideas I had caught the night before; but as I entered my room a martin was flying in front of an unfinished drop-curtain, attempting to light on the battlements of a castle in the painting. I could not work, try as hard as I might, and those ideas are yet unfinished."

It seems to me that he should have been flattered, instead of discouraged. That people will be hampered and fettered by imaginary evils is something very nonsensical. In an actor's life there are plenty of stern realities of an unpleasant nature, and it should be their study to give fancies the "go-by." By looking into the antecedents of Jonah companies, it is easily ascertained why they fail. A careful business man is the only one to manage successfully; and, however he may be looked

HUMPTY DUMPTY

at, or talked of by his company or outsiders, it is none of their concern further than they please their audience and get their salaries. We often hear agents and others speak of their managers as mean men; but I have noticed that the close and attentive man of business keeps salaries paid up, and has nothing to fear from "Jonahs."

If outsiders could look in, the charm for show business, as delineated by some traveling companies, would rapidly diminish, and be "nowhere." In a little town in Illinois, it happened that a concert company were short an agent, and the delay caused thereby was pleasantly filled in at a quiet little hotel, such as show folk like to strike. The town was enthusiastic on the "library question," and the managers congratulating himself on the good house given him, tendered the citizens a benefit in the "good cause." They jumped at it like a fish at a fly, and immediately set to work to raise an excitement. There were two playing at that game, they soon found; for a temperance "matinee" had commenced in order to buy out the only saloon in town, and the virtuous people therein were about equally divided. Of course, when a row starts, everybody is a privileged character; and the more fingers in the pie the better--or worse, as the occasion may be. First, the hall was pronounced unsafe by the temperance people, and they adjourned to the church for further meditation. Then the opposition declared that a church was no place for business matters, etc., etc. This was good enough in itself, but the "show folks" could not look on and see a row without a finger in, and they started. First, the star attraction quit and informed the manager to that effect. Then one after another took flight, until the manager was to be seen walking up and down the verandah of the hotel munching an immense chew of tobacco, and the treasurer biting his fingernails and delivering a general cussing to the female sex. The baggage was packed, and the manager quietly looked after its proper delivery at the depot. When all was up in arms, and all quietly and satisfactorily arranged by the manager, word was sent him by the "prima donna" that an immediate interview was desired in the parlor. Adding another potion to the chew of tobacco, he went to the parlor to find the company all gathered for a talk. They had the talk and concluded that they were in the wrong and wanted to keep on. Then the manager commenced to talk--a ghastly expression was on his face and swear words *ad infinitum* were in his mouth and in no way backward about coming out. In fifteen minutes the sky was clear and the company "smole sweet smiles" at one another, showing what a relief it was to get rid of so much cussedness. But on that manager's face were firm-drawn lines. With pencil in one hand and telegraph blanks in the other, he was talking with people in various parts of the country, and in a few hours there was formed another company, who were to meet at a designated point, and after all were cared for at the hotel, the manager called a meeting of the two companies in the parlor of the hotel, and on his face there was a look of severity rarely equaled. But on the faces of party No. 1 there were ghastly looks, subject to rapid changes.

MORAL:--Don't think, never mind how successful you may be, that you are the only attraction in the business, for no manager who has money at stake will ill-treat a company or misrepresent them; and further, no manager of any ability will be caught without something to turn to.

Cry them down! ye of immaculate virtue, who can bow your heads at the church altar, and ask you neighbor if your backhair is all right. Why do they go? Why is their curiosity worked up to the highest pitch? And why do you turn up your dainty noses at the lady (the nasty thing! you term it) who travels with a show? Can you answer it? Why, when you need a charity, do you go to the manager of a theatre, or to an actor, for it? Why should you expect charity, where you have none? Are you ever refused in a worthy cause? Never! And never will you be, so long as time lasts; for in no one does the heart beat so warmly for a brother in need as in the breast of a showman, and to no fraternity is the call oftener made.

A number of years ago a joint benefit was tendered to the Webb Sisters. At the conclusion of the entertainment they were called before the curtain and a speech was demanded by the audience. This was in Nashville, Tenn. One of them stepped forward and asked the question that heads this article. After a few graceful remarks, the phraseology of which I have at the present writing forgotten, the lady concluded with something like the following: "When a child, at my mother's knee, I learned to ask my heavenly father for his help and to thank him for favors so lavishly bestowed. Can I now, in the moment of success, thank him less?" You could have heard a feather fall in that crowded theatre, and many an eye was moist with sympathy.

Only a few days ago I went to a neighboring town to hear an entertainment by a traveling company. By invitation, I "took tea" with a friend of many years standing. He was a Methodist. Naturally, the conversation turned upon show people, and we were speaking of the entertainment given in the town some two years before by a company of which at the time I was a member, when the lady of the house remarked that but a day or two before a friend of hers had said, "That young man who played the fool (keen appreciation) is well connected, and ought not to disgrace his relatives." My answer was, "If the relatives don't find fault, why should a stranger?" And further, why should that stranger always be on hand to enjoy a hearty laugh, if he disapproves of such performances? O ye of little consistency! "Let him who is perfect among you cast the first stone."

During the late war I was compelled to remain over night in one of our Western cities, to make connection for the next stand. Agreeably to the wishes of the company, I went with them to one of the theatres. One of the members of the company was a general favorite, but at times given to a liberal use of "budge." It was one of his favorite characters that night, and I do not recollect ever having seen another so abject a failure on the part of an actor to delineate his part. I had never seen the party before and was dumb-founded to know the reason. Almost immediately I could hear the whisper so audibly passed through the house. "He's drunk, he's drunk!"

I noted the effect upon the actor--his face changed color, his eyes became moist, and with almost a feeling of despair he stepped down to the footlights, saying, "As much as you have to blame me for, ladies and gentlemen, tonight I am not intoxicated. I left the bed of my dying wife to fulfill my engagement here."

"Put out the lights!" "Drop the curtain!" "Go home! go home!" immediately came from a hundred throats, and in less than ten minutes the house was empty. It was a moment when the heart got the best of that accursed feeling that so generally exists.

But who had a word of sympathy for the bereaved actor, who arrived at his home just in time to see the smile of welcome on the face of the dying wife, and then to see the spirit return to him who gave it. I answer you--no one but the brother actor who always stands ready with hand and heart. And when the little funeral was passing through those broad streets, taking to its last resting place one they all loved, had the world been asked who it was, the answer would have been "Only a, showwoman!" But what says the Father above, who reads only the heart?

[*New York Clipper*, July 26, 1884]

⊗ ⊗ ⊗ ⊗ ⊗

Here is a sample of newspaper item we get very frequently of late:

> At the ----- Theatre last night a fearful panic (and probable loss of life) was averted by the coolness and presence of mind of the popular actor James Bluff. A part of the scenery caught fire, and the audience were about to rush out, when Bluff, with an assuring gesture, motioned the orchestra to play, and the house was quieted while the fire was promptly subdued.

It appears, then, that all an actor has to do in a case of this kind is to signal the orchestra to play. It doesn't seem, at first glance, a particularly intrepid and danger-defying act, and all those actors who are continually studying up how to be firm, collected and useful in trying occasions, to the end that their brave deeds may be properly blazoned to the world, would do well to digest this matter and keep themselves always in a position to be able to boldly signal the orchestra on the necessary provocation.

To be sure, an actor might do more good were he to smother an incipient fire, or throw water, or tear down the proper things; but as it appears to be customary to speak not so much of the practical party who does put out the fire as of the party who thoughtfully starts the music, why, certainly, a due regard for what the public want must be taken into consideration by the item-loving Thespian. In order that unanimity of purpose may exist in the band during a trying moment of excitement of this kind, and that a conglomeration of "sudden" music of any kind may not be wildly "pulled" on the fire--and the audience--it might be well for leaders to have an extra number added to their dramatic music books, marked "In Case of Fire"; and this music, it may not be necessary to remark, should be soothing and restraining to a large degree.

There is but one thing in this connection that causes uneasiness. If the fire should thoughtlessly begin to break out while the orchestra was playing, I do not see where the actor's chance would come in. He surely couldn't stop the orchestra. What would he do? Just the luck some actors would have. They'd be put out--if the fire wasn't. I really see no way, in the event of an occurrence like the above, to quiet the audience. I suppose the fire would have to burn, the audience have to become panicky, and some unlucky James Bluff be left again.

And speaking of theatrical fires and cleanings out, leads us to observe that there are some particular portions of the theatre devoted to performers that badly need a thorough and purifying burning. We allude to the majority of dressing rooms and music rooms throughout the country. Even in what are considered well kept theatres, the accommodations in this respect are miserable, while in a large number of so-called opera houses and town halls, wherein the traveling company most prevails, the condition of the rooms allotted to the performers for dressing purposes is shameful. In cold weather a lady is shown a miserable, dingy, dirty little imitation of a room, devoid of light or heat. The partition is liable to be full of generous sized peep holes--natural and artificial. In this bare and dusty space a lady is expected to undress, without fire, and with the pleasant prospect of having her "making-up" habits anxiously and feverishly gazed upon through the "vacancies" in the partition.

None but those who have traveled professionally would believe the indifference and neglect shown in this matter. The front of the house is well attended to and the public's welfare carefully provided for, yet the proprietors of these opera houses seem to give but little thought to the comfort or convenience of those whose entertaining powers are to produce the necessary pleasure and enjoyment--powers, by-the-bye, that would seem to be liable to a deal of change through the effect produced by comfortable or depressing surroundings.

If these proprietors would go up to their attic some cold night, search around for the most neglected corner, fence it up with planks sewed together with black thread, and then send their wives and daughters up there to dress, they would naturally be very soon in possession of excited information as to what human beings crave for in the trifling matter of necessary comfort and attention, and they would ever after think not too unkindly of the shivering little soubrette whom they hear violently--and possibly profanely--alluding to the niggardly characteristics of owners of suburban opera houses generally.

As to the matter of orchestral accommodation, the average, and indeed almost every, music room is a dirty, woe-begone snare and

TONY PASTOR

delusion. Even in city theatres, a bare room with wooden benches around the sides and with whitewashed walls is supposed to constitute a practical music room--a lonesome corner anywhere under the stage that suggests the dismantled barroom of a "dive." Outside of metropolitan houses the music room is a most damnable scheme. Very often it is no room at all, but a space formed by rolling away the dirt and debris of under-the-stage accumulations. In this imaginary room the traveling leader is often obliged to meet the local orchestra after the doors are opened in front; and, with all hands cramped, discontented and discouraged, the rehearsal must be waded through in the most expeditious manner.

But although dressing rooms and music rooms are thus apparently allowed to grow and get along the best way they can, it is worthy of remark that there are very often connected with these establishments some rather bright and well-appointed rooms in the front end of the building; but these belong to the proprietors--they are his offices and in these offices there does not seem to have been any difficulty in getting stoves in, or keeping them alight in wintry weather, while it is a remarkable fact that stoves in or near a dressing room never did know how to burn properly or last through the night without coal.

[*New York Clipper*, October 17, 1885]

❊   ❊   ❊   ❊   ❊

It is a curious fact that the average singer "just hates" to do a single turn. She feels much more contented when someone else is on the stage with her, some funny man who can do all the work and keep the audience genial and with whom she can shine with more certainty. For this reason the sketch team business has appreciable attractions for her. Besides this, the partner is of amazing usefulness in the matter of writing for dates, seeing to the trunks, skirmishing for the midnight sandwich and hunting up moderate priced laundries.

Even the use of professional slang has the power to determine the status of a performer. The artist who still insists that anything good is "great" or "immense" is looked upon with a pitying eye. Nothing but "up to the times" will now suffice for a term of praise or commendation. In like manner, the use of "made a hit with me" is acknowledged in conversation to be the proper thing. If Jimmy Brown did something or told something in a non-professional way that charmed you, do not remark afterwards, "Jimmy Brown knocked me out the other day, etc., etc.," but be professionally stylish and "up to the times" and confess that "Jimmy Brown made a hit with me the other day, etc., etc.," and then you can relate Jimmy's affair with all the confidence that comes of conscious propriety.

An aspiring composer was disheartened at the remorseless promptitude with which the manuscript of his first comic opera was always returned. A knowing friend explained. The first scene transpired during a rainstorm and the opening chorus was to be sung with umbrellas up. Stage superstition could not tolerate this. Only a band of yellow clarinets, all yellow clarinets, could have been worse. He is now willing up some sunshine for the scene.

The practical and thoughtful "mash" who will have baskets of flowers handed up to "the girls" will show his appreciation of a really good "pointer" by ordering hereafter, not natural, but French artificial flowers for the purpose--every way as charming and thrilling in effect, and by far more useful. Good for a long time for both professional and private adornment in connection with hair, dress., etc.

The Kazoo is the latest. It blooms principally, just at present, in Detroit, a music concern there seeming to fancy there is something in it. It is a wind instrument that comes in assorted sizes. On it can be produced, in cold blood, glaring imitations of the bagpipes, the cornet, the fiddle, the whistle, the leader, the caller and the brass band, besides its own distinctive Kazoo characteristics. It can be played alone or together. Twenty of it, with capes, caps and torch lights, will make a serviceable band for the political campaign. At least, that is what the Kazoo pictorial pamphlets insist on. The beauty of it is anybody can play it--man, woman, kid or baby--in just five minutes' time. Another beauty of it is, it only costs ten cents for a small one. There are large ones, as roomy as a trombone, which look very imposing, yet are still nothing more than big Kazoos. However much the Kazoo may be distressingly boomed into the moderately respectable musical ear, it is quite likely that might, for a while, serve as a little novelty in the musical moke acts of the variety stage.

The well-worn exaggeration, "He can just make that fiddle talk!" is only exceeded in downright nonsense and recklessness by the all-too-common expression, "He can play anything you put before him." To speak very, very mildly, it is something of a little job for the best of them to play "anything that is put before them" in an implacable hurry; and we are willing to stake three dollars that we are not using this week that quite a number out of every two of the best of them will be apt to get side-tracked in a hurry if the right party is "putting up" the music they are to scramble through.

It is the new "props" of a little traveling party--who also plays a modest young part--that writes home to his folks and to his girl that he likes the company first-rate, that he is acting in the play, and that the manager says he does as well as any of them; but who writes never a word, never an innocent little word concerning his trunk juggling duties or his bill peddling abilities.

It would be a difficult matter to explain why it is that female vocalists, serio-comic, burlesque and otherwise, so naturally take to singing the moment they leave their room and strike the halls and passages of a hotel. They conclude they will make a flying visit to someone else's room, and the moment they close their door it is ten to one they will immediately break out into easily heard vocal exercises till they reach their destination. Note this; and also note the strange fact that if they are going out, and are dressed, they do not sing. Let this claim your further attention and speculation.

There is a deal of dissatisfaction caused in traveling troupes by careless billing. Large quantities of programs, etc., are ordered at a time, by reason of the reduced figures allowed on large orders. These will surely be used up, no matter what changes may take place in the company, and the original cast will be read as long as a bill remains. It is, therefore, a common occurrence for a performer, who, perhaps, is making something of a hit in a part, to be obliged to see himself or herself represented as the one who formerly played the part--a state of things not at all encouraging to an earnest and painstaking professional.

Some philosophic German musicians, amazed at the increasing influx of Irish and English trombonists and cornettists of first-class quality, have been making a scientific study of the probable cause of this national tendency to good brass execution. "It must be a different kind of mouts ofer dhere!" is their solemn decision.

Comic opera companies--and worse still, Ideal Comic opera companies--and even still worse, New York Ideal Comic opera companies (if the billing be truthful) playing to ten-cent audiences in halls, not museums, should attract the thoughtful attention of every young and dreamy would-be *bouffe prima donna*, and cause her to hesitate before rejecting the offer of a man fully able to support and care for a wife, and lay his hand on a ten dollar bill or two once in awhile without energetic and desperate skirmishing.

"I don't care how soon I close. I never get left!" is too often the utterance of a party who hasn't the ghost of a chance to "catch on" suddenly anywhere. If performers would but rid themselves of this all too-common style of remark and get to understand that there is a deal of difference between true independence and cheap "bluff," much trouble and misery would be saved all around, and many good-natured friends would be spared numerous and disheartening "braces" for wealth, and quiet and inoffensive trunks would be spared the mortification and loneliness of being left behind in various hotels among strange and unfriendly baggage until they received their pardon.

It may be a consolation to some few professionals at the present time to hear that the fact of salaries being a long way behindhand is very often a positive benefit, since when there is no money in the clothes there is a rather slim chance of any being foolishly spent, and when the back salary does appear there is enough of it in a lump to do some good. This bit of philosophy we hope will prove cheering and sustaining. It just occurs to us, however, that if back salary does not appear at all, there is, candidly speaking, not so much benefit in having the manager slow in pecuniary affairs. In such a case, which we understand sometimes happens, we wish to take back everything we have said concerning the matter.

It must be terribly puzzling for a comedian to read that his play and his acting are tiresome and stupid, and yet be unable to prevent the yells of delight and satisfaction that nightly greet him and his presentations from contented and well-pleased audiences.

[*New York Clipper*, October 18, 1884]

⊛ ⊛ ⊛ ⊛ ⊛

The Happy Hottentots die hard. One would fancy that the marked similarity of the various Hottentot acts and their constant repetition would tend to render them monotonous to even the most patient auditor; but the act still seems to possess a weird charm for many, and its dark stage, mysterious contortions, realistic makeup, and lovely gibberish combine to yet attract rapt and profound attention, while its black-limbed and solemn high-kicking, to the monotonous and ever-recurring "tum, tum ter-ra-ra; tum, tum ter-ra-ra; tum, tum ter-ra-ra," of its instrumental interlude, repeated "till ready," continues to possess a strange fascination for audiences good-natured and accommodating enough to overlook the slight inconsistency of hearing two representatives of the simon-pure Hottentot converse in broken-Hottentot or something at the beginning of the act, and then easily swing into the every-day English of their Hottentot song.

Judgment, as well as musical ability, is necessary in the selection of the orchestral "overtures" at the theatre. A lack of this quality caused a leader at one of our principal theatres to play a medley composed entirely of songs relating to home for the first orchestral selection, the slightly well-known song of "Home, Sweet Home," being the main feature. No matter how sweet home may be, musically or practically, and, notwithstanding all the bosh that has been written about the musical reference to it by emotional souls the world over, the fact remains that it was rather out of place to pleasantly usher in an evening of contemplated enjoyment at the theatre by musically reminding everybody, with all the directness that brass, string and reed could combine to produce, that it should be ever borne in mind that there was no place like home, which little reminder would naturally cause one to feel that, howsoever pleasant even the theatre might be to the weary spirit looking for a little relief, there was really, and without exception or doubt, no place like home. Slightly discouraging this to the innocent visitor, and not quite so reassuring and comfortable as to hear a spirited quickstep, not too Prussian in its build, an ever-welcome and harmless Waldteufel waltz, not forgetting the encore-receiving xylophone for a breezy and rackety finale.

The straight-jig of the minstrel and variety theatres has given rise to a deal of daring and deliberate music among a certain class of composers, [so that] anything in the way of a popular song is now twisted and hurried into the necessarily nimble time of the jig, and the outsider in such matters would hardly realize that a song like "Sweet Spirit, Hear My Prayer," could, by any process, be made the good jig it can be. The "Pretty Girl Milking Her Cow," the "Last Rose of Summer," the "Miserere" from *Trovatore*--even the "Cujus Animam" of Rossini--have all been grappled by the remorseless jig-juggler and "slugged" into some sort of serviceable shape, one insanely-original music explorer having deliberately distorted the music of the *Doxology* into a joyous and heel-starting straight-jig. The stop-jig idea, where an occasional rest of a few bars occurs while the dancing is continued, thereby enhancing the general effect, is now being savagely improved and experimented upon, one pianist in a traveling company stopping entirely and leaving the piano, returning leisurely after a while to carelessly take up the jig almost anywhere. As the time must be paid strict attention to, even when not playing, it is not a bull to say that it takes a rather good musician to play these rests. As professional pride or ambition is limited to no one class of violinists, it may be noted in connection with this jig business that there are a number of violinists throughout the country whose lives are rendered considerably comfortable and satisfactory in the possession of a reputation for being "daddies" in straight, crooked, stop or go-as-you-please jig-playing; and almost any performer from the very distant West will be sure to tell you of some talented violin player out there who used to play his jigs all alone and just about "knock the tar out of 'em," which exhibition of decided genius would have undoubtedly boosted him up even with Remenyl, were it not for his unfortunate and uncontrollable habit of filling his violin with whiskey and drinking the accursed stuff from a leak in the end of his instrument while playing.

A majority of the specialty sketches for two people would seem to be constructed in this handy manner. Enter She. "Not here? Where is he?

Well, I'll have to sing a little song." Sings a little song and dances off into scenery. Enter He. "Not here? Where is she? Well, I'll have to sing a little song." Sings a little song. Enter She. "Ah! there he is." "Ah! there she is." Now begins the solid work. A few quarts of "chestnuts" will here be all that is necessary, for, say what you may, audiences will laugh at chestnuts. Then work up a quarrel, "get back" at each other in good shape, a little property "cry" from She, and property

remorse from He. "Will make up on one condition." "What is it?" "Sing a little song with me." "All right." They sing a little song—a little medley song, with Rooney and camp-meeting reminiscences. Off. Encore must be short and funny. Come on and bow to the audience backward, escaping hurriedly during the laugh, or watch the scene closing in behind you and look as if you were going to say something comical—and don't say it. The second encore is easy—for you will not get it! This style of sketch doesn't cost much and brings in salary enough to keep you continually traveling and hustling our lovely country.

[*New York Clipper*, January 3, 1885]

❀ ❀ ❀ ❀ ❀

Visitors to Philadelphia who have gone around to the beautiful new Temple Theatre and Musee, on Chestnut Street, have already complained of the inattention and apparent sullenness of one of the officers stationed near the boxoffice. They state that they have asked questions of this officer concerning the theatre and the musee, and have received no reply whatever. But they should be informed that the particular officer in question who is so uncommunicative really cannot help it, for he is a wax one; and howsoever natural he may be, so far as appearances go, he is quite unable to speak, since wax figure making has not advanced to that point as yet. Therefore must he be pardoned for not answering queries or paying the slightest attention to anxious conundrums of any kind.

Leader Zimmerman, of the Arch Street Theatre, Philadelphia, says that a popular minstrel leader, noted for his love of practical jokes as well as for his animated imitations of nature on a violin, that can also do very clever legitimate musical work, was once asked by a country fiddler how he extracted so fine a tone from his instrument. He might have said it was simply because he could, but he didn't say so. He told the verdant Paganini that the entire secret was contained in a certain scheme which he would "give away" to a brother violinist with pleasure. He said it was the violin, not the player, and the violin had to be prepared. It was necessary to soak it in sea water for one week, and then have it thoroughly dried in the sun for at least another week. That was all there was about it, but a secret worth knowing. It will be observed that the time required to develop this beautiful tone gave the disinterested giver of "pointers" ample time to get at least thirty-two bars from town before the country Cremona caught a deathly or ruinous cold.

Michael Brand, one of the very best musical directors in the country, is at his old post in the Cincinnati Grand Opera House.... Michael is the Thomas of the West, and, besides being on more than intimate terms with a violin and other emotional affairs, he caresses the mournful cello in a most scholarly way.

The night parade of the Order of Cincinatus, illustrating the poem of "Lalla Rookh," was a glowing novelty to many of the show folk temporarily located in Cincinnati. A few dozen immense cars--or floats, as they were termed--were used to properly give the open-mouthed multitude an idea of what Tom Moore was really driving at when he penned that little Lalla Rookh incident. To every car a very live band was attached, and the music illuminations and theatrical appearance of the moving scenes suggested an idealized edition of a Barnum Circus parade, wherein angels with mustaches were not the least uninteresting feature of the brilliant *tout ensemble*.

The Cincinnatus Ball at that wonder of splendid structures, the Music Hall, admittance to which was not entirely as easy as falling off the dear old log, was a high-toned, low-necked affair, that looked very up to the times--the fashionable times--and wound up the festivities in a blaze of the usual chestnuts. The *coup d'eil* was splendid (rare old vintage), and the fortunate guest might well make allowances for the beaming satisfaction of the members of the Order Cincinnatus. Yet, if the aforesaid fortunate guest had ever attended any of the grand N. Y. City affairs--the Liedenkranz, Arion or Purim balls, for instance--he would have been pardoned for making just a few trifling mental comparisons as to what was a really way-up, two-band sort of an affair, anyhow. And still there were decidedly "no flies, nohow, by no manner of means," on the Cincinnatus revelry, and whoever says there were wasn't there.

The Sain-Saens orchestral work, the "Danse Maccabre," has caused many weird and hushed opinions among musicians as to its ghostly beauty. Verily, Sainty struck an originality when he "thought up" this particular Dance of Death. Old Nick himself is supposed to get out his violin and play for the dance of the "deaders." At the first sound of a strain of really devilish rhythm and suggestiveness, the dead ladies and gentlemen are supposed to "hands all 'round" in a grimly festive step. The xylophone, heretofore principally of use to wind up popular melodies of the day, is called upon to musically illustrate the idea of skeleton dancers, the tone being expected to suggest the movements of hilarious and restless bones. Altogether, the effect is startling and shivery, and when the cock crows and the bony guests hurriedly seek coffin seclusion, the listener "comes to" with eager satisfaction, and carries with him but as a dream the funny effect of a remarkable musical work.

Herman Leopold still goes around every night to the People's Theatre, "Over the Rhine" in Cincinnati, to see the performance. While watching the entertainment he pleasantly passes the time playing a violin down near the stage with some quiet-looking musical friends, who, somehow or other, always seem to succeed in finding front--very front seats--no matter how crowded the house.

[*New York Clipper*, October 31, 1885]

⊛ ⊛ ⊛ ⊛ ⊛

"Backcapping" is the bane and curse of professional circles. It prevails everywhere, and, unlike open and forcible aggression that can be met and contended with, its terribly destructive work goes on in silence, and--in the majority of cases--without the slightest knowledge of its victims. Every professional in the country knows to what an extent this cruel talk is daily and hourly carried on, and too many know to their sorrow how powerful is its ability to work evil results. In dressing room, in saloon, in street, in train, and--delicious opportunity--in hotel room after performance, this "backcapping" specialty is constantly going on.

The out-and-out declaration of one's opinions, cowardly though it be to abuse an absent one, is not so bad as the quiet, plausible method of breathing gentle insinuations. There is a type of female professional (that every performer will readily recognize) that can cause more general trouble in a company than a regiment of nervous landlords and businesslike constables. A representative of this type will seldom commit herself by plainly proclaiming her likes and dislikes. She is too "discreet" for that. She has had "experience," has suffered, and knows-- or fancies she knows--just how best to make her shots tell. She is generally "nice;" a very "nice" young person, indeed--or a very "nice" old young person, indeed--who is capacious as to witching smile and expressively innocent as to business ogle. With a "practicable" tongue she timidly ventures to call attention to the mysterious fact that so-and-so and so-and-so is the case. The rapt attention she at once receives startles her by its eagerness, and she begs that she will not be misunderstood feels faint, and beseeches a glass of water, if you please, though sherry will do.

The excitement subsiding, she starts in again, and makes matters worse by tearfully calling upon someone present to back her statements by frankly confessing that he or she has noticed that so-and-so was really the case. Some addle-brained he or she mildly assents that, "come to think of it, things did really look that way," and so the sociable work proceeds. The gentle "backcapper" retires with her reliable tongue and diseased heart, and the trouble is well under way.

It is hardly necessary to enlarge on the fact that the habits and customs she so greatly deprecates in others are tolerably certain to have very often made themselves a part and parcel of her own "experiences." "Nasty-nice" is not pretty, but still an all-meaning designation for these parties; who, however--in the evolution of a just retribution--rarely succeed, despite all their artifices and petty tricks, in bettering themselves or getting up and out to a position which does not require trick and artifice to maintain.

There is also a type of male demon who will be speedily recognized by professionals everywhere. This particular demon organizes himself into a sleepy tableau before a bar, gets full, grows "talky," and gains the immediate attention of the hangers-on by his various stories concerning performers' business, secrets, and general morals. With this specimen no woman's character is safe, and the delectable morsels of gossip roll from his stupid tongue in rapid succession, heedless of the misery and trouble they may create when the listeners shall have confidentially but industriously circulated the pleasing rumors until they have finally reached the proper ears. The open avowal, the dastardly insinuation, the suggestive hint, the quiet "pointer," all tell alike to the greedy ears of the hearers; even a bit of expressive silence is not misunderstood--as it was not meant to be.

Then there is a world of "backcapping," in a smaller way in which the expressions "really thinks he is great," "rotten," "yaller," "N.D.G.," "too much paint in her white-wash brush," "married again?

gracious, where's the last?" "was good, but getting much tart." "takes here, cause it's his town." "gall of galls," "brazen old chippy," "oh, no, he ain't fresh," "seventy-five what a week?" "remember when they played for fifteen for the four," "closed in on 'em in Boston first night," "keeps there, cause he works for nothin" "better buy a new voice," "did you see her eye next mornin'?" "getting coarse, I should say so," "very ochy-coochy," "wrote nothin'," "worked up the gallery," "he took that from me," "what is she made up for?" etc., etc., etc., are as plentiful as drum-bangs in a big-four dance. This state of things does not speak well for professional human nature, but we all recognize the fact that the statements are in no way exaggerated.

Curiously enough, there is another class who never speak a word against anybody, and still are almost as bad as the others; for in their desire to be thought dear, good souls, they make a point of praising and excusing everybody, and even their surprisingly good-natured words have a contrary effect from that which was intended, when the purpose of their loving expressions is fully understood.

The trials and troubles incidental to professional work are surely plentiful enough without having the general unrest added to by idle tales, unnecessary interference or prejudicial criticism; and if any of these words of ours shall touch the consciences of the old offenders, or reach the yet reclaimable hearts of the newer ones, and cause them to see that there is nothing but trouble for both sides in the practice of this harassing habit, then this article shall not have been written in vain, and a little more of cheerful good-fellowship and encouraging tolerance may possibly enter into and brighten up the round of professional existence.

Why it is I cannot explain; but it is true, nevertheless, that the feeling entertained for show people by the world at large is covered by the time-honored expression, "Take in the clothes, mother; the show has come." That there are many graceless specimens of humanity connected with it, none will dispute; but is the proportion any greater than in other branches of business? Possibly the reason is that they are placed under closer observation than any other class, and the world is inclined to look for the bad points, forgetting the good. Each and every show company is a little world by itself. It has all the peculiar dispositions, and has them placed in such a way that the bad side shows first. It has its ups-and-downs, it has its professional grumblers, it has its jovial good-fellows, and it has its jealousies. The last phase, I regret to say, is predominant. It is, however, only human nature, and none but an unreasonable man would expect any machine to run without oiling, for it would grate and grind on its bearings until they were worn out and broken down. Courtesy and a little wholesome flattery are perhaps as good an oil as you can use.

Seldom you find intimate friends in a traveling company; it may be different in stationery enterprises, but certainly traveling together brings no balm to the tired brain and worn body. Let sickness interpose her unwelcome hand and the change is like magic. Hearts that beat only for self heretofore are open wide to the sufferer; and be he never so small a spoke in the wheel, he commands the willing assistance of one and all. Petty foibles are forgotten, jealousies are laid aside, and there arises a friendly strife to see who shall do the most to assuage the pain and encourage the sufferer. One heart beats in all, and that is a noble one, filled with good and holy thoughts, which have an escape only under such circumstances.

Here you see the heavy man, who makes his audience learn to look upon him with scorn, smoothing the pillow of the sufferer with all the tenderness that he can conjure up--thinking, perhaps of that mother who made his pillow more comfortable than anyone else ever could. Here, too, is the comedian, who we never think of except as the jolliest being of all, quietly fanning, with a sober face; and, perhaps, if you notice closely, you will see a moisture about the eyes that looks strangely where you have only seen sparkling humor. All are ready and waiting to extend a helping hand.

If the sufferer recovers, how naturally they drift back to the old ways and their indifference to another's welfare; but should death claim as its own one who has been a companion in joy and sorrow, it awakens another feeling, and they all look toward one another for comfort and sympathy. Gentle are the words that speak of the favors and little pleasures that have been received at the hands of him who has now "gone on" for the last time. Perhaps some member of the company tells some little incident of thoughtful consideration in the past, that none but him may have noticed. But now all think of it, and in recalling that there comes many another, until the dead is made a hero of, although until taken away he had, perhaps, not been appreciated as such. None of his faults are recalled, and how closely his fellows seem bound together for the time being. So seldom is sympathy extended from the outside world, that they learn not to look for it there; but if it comes,

and sometimes it will, from an unexpected source, how it is welcomed, and what a noble being this outsider seems!

I recollect an instance that occurred near a little town in New Hampshire. Business had been "queer" for some time and the last "chuck" had been broken (for crackers and cheese). Tired and hungry, our little party plodded along the dusty road, when a good-natured farmer offered us a ride to our next stand. That man was a god in our eyes, and how warmly thanks were given as he left us at the hotel! He came in that night to the show (by invitation), bringing his family, and was so completely "mashed" by the bone-player that he went home with his pocketbook five dollars lighter, and the bone-player went home the next morning disgusted with what fancy had painted as a paradise. He had made a mistake in his calling--that was all; and when I last saw him, a blue-and-gold sign hung in front of a nicely stocked drygoods store, and on the sign was the name of my old comrade. Such is life. We can't all be bone-players, nor can we all be drygoods men. But such as falls to our lot let us take up with a willing hand, and try to elevate in such a manner that when the "main guy" above gives us the "cue" we can catch the line and "go on" with a well-studied part. What did you say? How much? Fifty cents for adults, twenty-five cents for children.

[*New York Clipper*, August 9, 1884]

❀ ❀ ❀ ❀ ❀

And there are, then, "kickers" in professional circles? Well, yes, there very rarely are not, sometimes! A company without a "kicker" would appear unnatural, not to say highly irregular; and if everything went along smoothly and sociably, something terrible would happen, without a doubt. There is such a thing as being too good, and there is such a thing as a company agreeing entirely too well among themselves. Such a course would violate all the precedents and respected traditions of the business. Whether it is the natural jealousy of performers, the "mashing," the irregularities, or the abundance of idle time that causes all the turmoil, it is hard to say; but certain it is that the "kicking" propensity exists in a very robust and assertive state of health in the average theatrical troupe, and that the harsh efforts of managers and the mild measures of peacemakers alike have failed to more than subdue it for the time being. The general "kickers," as their name implies, are ready to tackle anything that affords a chance for a growl. They are not limited to any special grievance, and will kindly discover a quarrel in anything from a reduction of salary or a discharge, to a request to have baggage ready before breakfast. Their never-failing statements that when they were with the Buck and Sockskin Show they never were imposed on in such a manner, and that old Carats, manager of the Carrie Carats Company, would sooner cut off his left tongue than ask his "people" to do anything of that kind, and that, in the "Ten Days in a Shirt" Combination, playing eight distinct parts was always rewarded by a noticeable increase in salary, and that the manager of the "Thirty-Three Graces" never bothered his head about the private affairs of his company, so long as they properly attended to their professional work; and all such constantly repeated bits of information are always brought bravely to the front to contribute their share to the impending trouble and to invite hasty and decided remarks concerning the general worthlessness of Buck and Sockskin, old Carat, "Ten Days in a Shirt" snaps and "Graces" fakes of all descriptions.

Among the special "kickers," the hotel fault-finders are entitled to prominent mention. Hardly as the company arrived at the hotel before a voice (fully up to the concert pitch) is heard on the second floor front, shrieking bits of opinion on the laying-out of rooms to the manager, the clerk and the occasional chambermaid. It is the voice of Miss St. Jack. She is saying that it is always the way--she never knew it to fail--her room always looks out over a chimney garden, and Miss Smiles always has a front room with all the modern eccentricities, just because the treasurer of the company thinks he's her cousin, which everybody knows he isn't, and never will be. Then Quizby in a trot-moonish sort of way growls from the sixth floor that he'll be eternally something or other if he is going to be mistaken for an old trunk and sent up in the garret in every ten hotels out o' nine, and sarcastically gives it as his unbiased opinion that "doubling up" means two in a bed, and not four.

This hotel-complaining, however, is pretty much done away with by the pay-your-own-board system, whereby Miss St. Jack can have the frontest room in the house, and Quizby can sleep in two beds at once, providing they pay for the accommodation.

The table "kicker" is another delightful demon. A girl who has been boiling coffee over a gaslight and eating tomorrow's toast in a furnished room previous to joining the troupe, will be very likely to frown in the voice if there is no wishbone in her dish of frogs-legs; and the dignified gent who, after an interesting--though possibly brief--experience at beer and Saratoga chips of bologna, is solidly fixed before a real table of real food, will be very apt to wear a tragic eyebrow and orate with anger if the turkey has apparently been detained too long on earth to suit the delicacy of his "show." The quality of the meats is "pie" for these "kickers," and all the dear old funnyisms and ironical points are trotted out with unfailing regularity to do duty as reminders to hotel landlords and scheming waiters that people who know the difference between cow and mule are eating.

Even a change of seats at table is a delicious opening for a quiet riot "on the side." "Can't see why I can't have same seats I had all day yesterday. Guess I'm of as much importance as anybody else."

A delay in being waited on adds fuel to the fire. "Guess they're waiting for me to give them passes. But they'll get none from me. Here, waiter (angrily), bean soup! with (sarcastically) BEANS IN!"

And then there are some of them--generally the little darlings of the show--who will growl because there is nothing left on the table wherewith to extemporize a sneak sandwich in a napkin, to utilize after the show at night with the evening beverage.

The drinking "kicker" is possibly the worst of all. Always late, and always ready to resent any allusion to his tardiness; always "talky," and not disposed to have any of his thoughtful remarks objected to; always stubborn in regard to who is right and who is wrong, from a dispute with the barkeeper about who paid for the round before the last, to a difference of opinion with the manager concerning the brilliant effects of drink upon an actor's stage work--it is no wonder that he succeeds in making himself and everybody else suffer from the "ideas" that staggers through his vaporing head; and it is no wonder, either, that, in consequence of all this detraction from other and more important matters, the manager of the present prefers the reliable man, even though not quite so good professionally, to the more gifted one who, by reason of his irregularities and "peculiarities," is the source of so much downright trouble socially, and so much unevenness professionally.

The race of music "kickers," it is comforting to note, is slowly but surely dying out. The older performers indulge in it but seldom, having long ago discovered the false light it placed them in to attribute to the music the reason for an audience's lack of appreciation; the "new ones," however, appear to run naturally to it at first, until a bit of common sense, or a friendly "pointer" from some older hand, leads them

not to complain until there is decided cause for complaint. The few who must "kick" are not at all dangerous, since most of their positive and entirely one-sided statements are made in the wings or in the dressing rooms, localities where all such mouthings have been time and oft before, and where such utterances are appreciated exactly at their full value.

Exaggeration would seem to be one of the things necessary to a complete professional outfit, and, in many cases, exaggeration is, to put it mildly, a decidedly polite and circumspect word for it. It doesn't appear possible for the average performer to tell the exact truth concerning professional subjects unless it be entirely unavoidable. Salaries, "hits," engagements, all are exaggerated to an extent that brings the statements perilously near the field of downright lying, and many of them get right there--and stay there. In regard to salaries, it is our humble opinion that the truth is never told except where fibbing would be hopelessly absurd. In terse Saxon, they lie by the yard about it, with a few exceptions, which is always safe to add in broad statements of this kind. Not dark and dastardly lying, true enough, but decided deviations from the strict line of veracity. If these figures deceived anyone, there might be some pretext for their use; but, since the fraud is readily distinguished, a mental reduction in the figure is quickly and quietly made by the hearer, and something at least near the amount is soon arrived at.

In regard to "hits," the legitimate's "the house rose at me, me boy!" and the specialist's "knocked 'em cold, pards!" are alike well known and well understood. In like manner, "Barrett was sick that night, and I was called upon to play his part at three minutes' notice. The audience never knew the difference, me boy, and Barrett got well at once"; and "my turn came seventeenth on the bill after all the big cards, and, honest cull, I held the house and made the hit of the show. Ask the gang"--both fail of their objective, since they are entirely too familiar in texture to properly amaze anyone who has been hearing professional shop-talk for any length of time.

In regard to salaries, a reliable arithmetical scheme would be to divide the amount stated to have been received by four or three, according to the speaker's volubility, and the actual amount will be nearly ascertained.

A peculiar point deserving attention is that among really large-salaried professionals there is a tendency, when speaking of their earlier

salaries, to go to the other extreme, and get the figures away down.
"Fact, me boy; in the Spring of 18--, I played in that same house for six
small cases a week." The smallness of the former figure, compared to
the improvement in the later salary, never fails to cause the latter to
seem much more extensive and mammoth.

There is no limit to the stories set afloat by the apparently
comfortable habit of exaggeration. This, for instance:

"So you've left that company, eh?"

"Yes."

"How was that? Didn't you suit?"

"Suited too well! That little part they gave me I played so well
and made so much of that the star had no chance when I was on; so he
got mad, and discharged me for omitting a comma in one of my
speeches one night."

And the little party who was excused from further business relations with the company, owing to her habit of prolonging her suppers
with her friends until after matinee time next day, gets everybody saying, "Left them? Of course I did! Why wouldn't I? The star got awfully
jealous because that little side step of mine on my first exit used to
catch the house and spoil her next entrance. She was just no good after
that little step of mine, for all her imported wig and silk tights. My
little old red stockings and that side step caught on every time; and Mr.
Cluster, who is in a bank or something, and Colonel Guff, who is in the
Regular Marines or something, and Dr. Services, who is in a college or
something, all said that I was the attraction; and they ought to know,
for they know every lady in the business, and are posted on everything.
They advise me to get an author to write a new play around that side
step of mine, and then star--and I'm going to!"

If a specialty-vocalist sings but two songs, there is always a
lovely amount of exaggeration in the excuses. "Could have sung three,
but wouldn't." "Didn't want to--tired, anyway." "Orchestra drowned
me," "Monday night's bad here anyway." "Cold audience always in
Coalhole; they like it, but don't applaud much." "Miss Trigamy only
sang one song when she was here, the stage manager tells me," and so
on.

In this field of exaggeration, when two "Greeks meet," then indeed is a "tug-of-war"--of lies.

"How much did you pay for de super, pards?"

"Twenty-five cases, cull."

"Twenty-five? Why, you got yours cheaper than mine. I had to pay four-and-a-half cold cash for mine!"

I not long ago had occasion to visit a professional lady on business matters connected with her songs. A clipping from a paper printed in the bills read:

To a bright and charmingly ingenuous face of softest beauty and an undulating loveliness of form and figure is added a velvety, luscious voice attuned to a deliciously low and soft articulation," etc., etc., etc.

I went to the house where all this lived. Something tired looking and the reverse of giddy let me in.

"Who's that, mom?" came the shrill question from something leaning over the stairs. "All right. Be down in a minute."

It came down. It must have just got up or was possibly asleep yet. It wore a wrapper of the medieval ages and the slipperless foot was the one that had a shoe on it. There was recklessness in its hair, jaggedness in its eyebrow-curves, and biliousness in its complexion. Some of last night's applause still remained on the side of her nose, while her black eyelashes had leaked through the night and streaked at right angles down and across her desperately sweet, catch-anybody smile. When I had gone I re-read the paper's notice, and then I was forced to admit that press agents also do occasionally deal in exaggeration of a certain kind.

[*New York Clipper*, September 6, 1884]

        ✪   ✪   ✪   ✪   ✪

"One of the showmen, ain't you? I thought so. I can always tell 'em. Where do you show next? Hell's Hole, eh? Right good little town. You'll have a big house there. Hell's Hole folks always turn out and fill the operry house whenever something good comes along. Where'd you show last? Jayburg, eh? Bad house? Yes, I s'pose you had. Dead town, that. Nothin' but a circus catches Jayburg.

"Had a kinder light house here last night, that's so; but that's nothin'. First night always bad. You'll have a crowded house tonight. The boys all say the show gave great satisfaction. They say nothin' better ever struck the town. Don't mind last night. You see, everything was against you. The lumbermen are on strike, and so there was no wood to keep the parlor-match factory running, and a couple of

hundred girls that always take in the show were out of work on that
account. Besides, there was a dance over at Ike Gristie's, and the
Methodist Church had a ham sandwich party last night. But tonight you
can't get 'em in. Eh? No, I don't mean that way. I mean you can't get
'em all in. I saw a feller this mornin' from Mudroads, fourteen miles
from here, and he says he's comin', sure.

"Be you the feller that took off the Dutchman? I thought you
was. I can always tell 'em. You ain't, eh? Why, no; you're the Irishman that swung the chillaylee, or whatever you call it. I knew it was
you. No! Oh, yes; I see, leader of the orchestra. Well, you're a slick
one at it, you are. I'd like you to get acquainted with Doc Gall. He's
our leader here in town. He keeps the blacksmith shop across the road
there, and he's away up, first-class, bang-up--just like you. He can play
in operry in York, if he wants to, but his horse shoein' trade is good,
and he hates to leave the boys. He makes his own fiddles and strings,
and Happy Budd Gags, the big minstrel, tried to get him last season.
He can just make the fiddle speak in three languages, and he can play
when he's asleep.

"Want some bay rum? Johnny Bones, you know him, said he
never struck a shop with such square bay rum. No? All right. Next season.

"That there Dutchman you got with you is pooty good, but we
got a chap in town here who is no slouch at it, you hear me. Mebbe
you've seen him around Zeke's saloon this mornin'. I know he could be
coaxed to go with you, and you can get him mighty cheap. He's got an
awful funny new Dutch song called 'Lawterbach,' and you'd just die to
hear him say 'Nix cum arouse, is dot so!' Kinder keep an eye open for
him.

"Then there's Rube Schemmerhorn that keeps the grocery, he
takes off an Irishman first-rate. He came very near going with the Kuri-
ous Komedy Kompany lately. He did his Irish business with them for
one night on trial, and the manager said if there was anything else he
could do, even the slightest bit of anything else except the Irish
business, he would have some chance to go with his troupe. So you see
Rube came very near going. Hair tonic? Billy McCardigan, the great
clog dancer--you know him--said when he played here that he never
struck such bang-up, reliable hair tonic. No? All right. Some other
season.

"That nigger comedian of yours is tol'ably good, too; but, honest, there's a feller that slouches round town a good deal that's the party you want. He's the very cut of a real old Georgy darky, and he's got splendid big tips for the business, and a mouth that he can screw up into any shape. He burns his own corks, even makes his own corks, and when he's all fixed out, turns out his lips and says, 'Ay! golly!' You ought to hear the girls just scream. All he wants in the world is a comical wig and a pair of funny old pants with a laughable red patch on the knee.

"Cosmetic? Harry DeCourey, the great actor--you know him--said he never came across better cosmetic than.... No? All right. Some other year.

"How many's in your troupe? 'Steen, eh? That's what they always tell me. 'Chestnuts,' is that what you call it? Oh! I'm 'fly' every time. Say, who is that there girl that sung the songs about love, the one that had the short blue dress on? Miss Glones, eh? Curious name, ain't it? Well, she's just about as good as they make 'em. There ain't a girl in this town that can come to touch her, and her voice'll catch me every time. She's right handsome, too, ain't she? She's young too, ain't she? She ain't married, is she, or ain't she? I suppose everybody is kinder noticin' her, ain't they? She's a darlin', now, and no mistake. Gosh! but you fellers must have nice times travelin' around this way. I s'pose you're all well acquainted with each other in the troupe. What hotel do you stop at? Is that girl's mother with her? I'm goin' to the show again tonight just to see her. I'll applaud her every time. Kinder tell her it's me.

"Boots blacked? Minnesota Mick, the cowboy--you know him --when he was here last with the Insane West Show, said he never knew before what boot-blacking meant, and.... No? All right. Some other visit.

"Say, you haven't got a pass about you, have you? No? All right; I thought mebbe that.... Yes, I know the seats are on sale at Codliver's drugstore, but I thought.... Thought wrong, eh? All right.

"Say, partner, you fellers must get paid good big wages, don't ye? About how much, if it's a fair question, do they pay you a month?

None of my d---- business, eh? Well, you needn't get airy. I'll git the boys to queer your show tonight, see if I don't."

[*New York Clipper*, November 8, 1884]

⊛ ⊛ ⊛ ⊛ ⊛

Two "clean old men" on "the strings," a girl at the piano with the pleasant task of evolving a respectable accompaniment from second viola copies, and a twelve-year-old boy glued to the end of a cornet constituted the orchestra that was "pulled on" the amazed leader of a traveling company down South lately. And he was voted "real mean" because he would insist that something was wanting, and would sigh for a little jewsharp, or even a kazoo, to help him out.

The leader who roams around through the length and breadth of our country will find that at many of the rehearsals of the one-night-stands he will be expected to teach, as well as rehearse, the orchestra. "Right here we want a discord." And right there some one in the orchestra will be sure to say, "Oh, we're good at that!" The "chestnut" never remains unsaid--that is, most never.

The orchestra at Bidwell's Academy of Music, New Orleans, have been playing together, with one exception, for about eighteen years in the same house, the drummer having played but ten consecutive seasons. Some have been playing there longer than the above time, the viola player having been "seconding" away for twenty-seven years. Leader J. B. Vogle naturally takes a great pride in his "old boys."

Currier's Band from Cincinnati will probably take but little interest hereafter in Southern melodies after their late New Orleans experience. A season's engagement at the Exposition with presumably delightful surroundings was ruthlessly "cut" to an anxious three weeks' experience, during which schemes to obtain salary drove away all visions of Southern enjoyment. Some of the men came from New York, Boston, Philadelphia and other eastern cities, and the extra loss they incurred will serve to make them the wrong parties from whom to get a deliciously glowing picture of "away down South."

The timpanist (same salary as drummer) of the New Orleans Academy of Music amuses himself during his leisure moments by making canes of music paper. He has one cane made entirely of a manuscript copy of "Der Freischutz." Some years ago, when we thought we were "funnier" than we think we are now, it would have been an impossibility for us to have let this item go without touching on a rare set of "wheezes" about a man necessarily walking in time, or on time, or behind time, with one of these music canes; but now, as you will kindly notice, we say never a word about it. Build 'em up yourself.

It was told as an actual fact by a Southern leader that some years ago a certain minstrel violinist now dead procured an engagement in his orchestra through a friend of the management. This friend informed the leader that the violinist in question wasn't exactly an Ole Bull, but was such a good sort of fellow that it would give satisfaction to retain him if it could be done. The friend kindly admitted that the violinist couldn't read music at first, or second, sight, but proclaimed him to be the reel and jig fiddler of the country, bar none. The obliging leader solved the problem by having two bows for the unassuming violinist, one of which was for the unassuming violinist, one of which was greased. When the overtures, etc., were "on," the greased bow worked away in industrious silence; but when jigs and reels were necessary, the legitimate bow quivered to good purpose and the stranger was seen and heard. We hated to spoil the story, but had to ask how it was that the grease from the tricky bow didn't come off on the strings and thus render useless the workings of the playing bow. But the leader is telling that story yet, without the possibility of a doubt, notwithstanding our mean interruption.

And now the South comes in with her claimants for the honor of starting the Elks. Some few of our readers may have heard just a little discussion as to the authorship of certain "Beautiful Snow"; and a majority of the songs composed by performers of the present day have had such a number of author claimants as to cause bewildering doubts as to the original "matter." The authorship of the "North Pole" is another mystery, we believe. But all these cases sink into insignificance compared with the important question as to who was the very, very first to "start the Elks." It is astonishing how many performers and musicians there are throughout our land who insist that they were the originators of that solid and prosperous body. They all tell the same tale of how they first thought of it and gave their ideas to someone else, and then how, in a little back room somewhere, a few of them met and founded a club that developed into the present successful and respected association. "Why, sir, I am the man who started the Elks years ago with Charley Vivian" is getting monotonous, and if all these claims were true the Jolly Corks must have been a mammoth and "numerous" success from the start, and Military Hall on the Bowery, "Mammy Gieseman's," or various other unpretentious places couldn't have held them with either comfort or safety.

A New Orleans landlady, inflated with Exposition ideas, and possessed with the correct notion that "actors" have plenty of money they cannot use, is at present slaughtering professional stomachs at two dollars a day for five-dollar-a-week "board and lodging." Nothing to eat after four o'clock in the afternoon until breakfast at nine next morning, although, if you are hungry, she will kindly recommend some restaurant. The dessert consists of an orange and a doughnut. The "gang," disheartened after the failure of their hopes of getting enticing food in the "Paris of America," where so much good food can be found, go through the dinner act in silence, and then call the girl and meekly say, "Give us our doughnut, please." And the outsider, who hasn't the advantage of being professionally connected and of getting favorable rates everywhere, innocently lives on promises of succulence and quality, and really doesn't know enough to pay more for what he is getting.

And even down in Louisiana they tell the same dear old story of the leader who was so full of liquids before the show that he couldn't even find his way to--or from--the barroom to the orchestra; and yet, when he sat in his chair and started in with the orchestra, he seemed to "straighten up" instantaneously, and carried everything through without missing a note--not even a single note. And yet there have been cases where jovial leaders in this condition have not instantaneously "straightened up," and have not been above playing a "hurry" for a sentimental scene; and, indeed, we know positively of one case where the delightfully happy leader went into the orchestra with his bow--and left his violin in the music room.

With the recollection of many a pleasant evening passed in the various "Varieties," "Comiques" and "specialty" opera houses of all sorts throughout the country, and with the catching ring of their popular melodies buzzing in my ears and unconsciously swaying my susceptible feet, I open the budget and discuss the merry "show folks." Here is Jennie Hughes, not quite so ethereal, perhaps, as in the old Killarney days, but still energetic, ambitious and attractive; and--let me whisper it--ample to a cheerful degree. In wardrobe she varies from the sumptuous train of a parlor balladist and bouffe-vocalist to the attractively abridged full dress of a French Spy. Here are Maggie Weston, dark eyed and contented, with an occasional male specialty, and a dramatic line of general usefulness; Lizzie Conway, as vivacious and sprightly soubrette-ically as she is acceptable and pleasing vocally; Hindle, petite, neat and artistic; May and Flora Irwin, picturesque and interesting; Emily Sylvester, ladylike, dignified and deeply contralto; and Fannie Beane, with the aesthetic fan and the charmingly restless feet. Miss Fannie does some exceptionally good foot calisthenics in addition to her vocal work; and if she will publicly insist that her slightly crimson-tinted and golden-blush locks are red, why, she has no one to blame but herself if people come to believe it. The very unconventional Minnie Clyde sings and chats to her auditors as if she enjoyed it--as they certainly do. Miss Minnie seems marvelously at home on the boards, and faints but little from stage fright. Her "Clicquot" song is realistic enough to make a man thirsty, while her German has the pure Rhinewine flavor. Little Lizzie Derious and Georgie Lingard--about the size of quarter-notes--look like variety ingenues, while the blonde Lottie Grant, fair and comfortable, suggests a take-the-world-easy disposition of the most pronounced type. Maggie Bursell does some very agile rope-dancing, and Alice Bateman kicks roulades of clear-cut rhythm from her clever sabots. Lulu Delmay seems to be in a fair way to renew her "Dreamy Waltz" triumphs, while Katie Cooper, the latest, has "caught on" in her new line with encouraging celerity. Fannie Davenport rejoices in being female baritone and in possessing a voice of wondrous depth and rotundity. Carrie Howard, pretty and popular; Lou Sanford, experienced and easy; and Fanny Bernard, industrious and persevering, warble their ballads, waltz-songs, medleys and camp-meeting oratorios in a manner ever pleasing to their audiences, and, it is to be hoped, profitable to themselves.

On the other side we have Jerry Cohan, a successful "Molly Maguire," as well as a philosophic dancing-master; Harry Clarke, with a gossiping Talking Hand and a North-of-Ireland talking tongue; Paddy Murphy, short in the limb, but long in the voice, and a dancer who dances as if he meant business; Dan Nash, versatile and useful, equally at home in a jig, a song, a recitation and a coffee-pot fantasia; Acton Kelly, a quiet "Barney of Hibernicon" fame, widely known and appreciated in his line; and the Emerald Four, neat and rough by turns, and ever ambitious and persevering--all awakening liveliest reminiscences.

Here we have Larry Tooley, the popular "vet," and Sailor West, the "new 'un." The Sailor sings well and is not at all motionless in that hornpipe. Had he but a leg or two more, he would accomplish wonders. Kerrigan, the good-looking piper, can certainly get out whatever music may be contained in a bagpipe. This instrument with orchestral accompaniment is something of a novelty, but it works in roaring style, and the foot that doesn't beat responsive to the music when one of those old reels is under way is either a churchfoot or a wooden one. Don Ferreyra, the bills assure us, is a man-flute. He does some very artistic whistling. How he does it--whether by the aid of finger-holes in his thumb, a steam calliope in his mouth, or a nice little flute up his nose--I don't pretend to know. He blows out lots of operatic music in a mysterious way, and apparently doesn't tire easily.

But here is a natural-born mimic, if ever there was one--Frank Bush, if you please, proprietor and inventor of those Hebrew hands, possessor of that atrociously grotesque dialect, and patentee of the Bush gesture. Francis, in addition to his specialties, imitates schoolboys, old maids, Hebrew geese, tin whistles, dead horses, broomsticks, quartets, brass bands, sandwiches, invisible ink, mustard (both French and German), safety pins, measles and dark rubber overshoes. Indeed, there is nothing that he would not delight in undertaking to imitate for you; and it would be very likely to please you, and be certain to please him.

Like poets and soft-shell crabs, these natural mimics are "born, not made." Like the good-natured Ned Barry, the ever-attentive Pat Reilly is as clever at scene-painting as he is at vocal eccentricities, and, possessing as he does a deal of perseverance and practical sense, is not apt to "get left" to any dangerous degree.

Orndorff and McDonald, and also Tommy Watson, may be numbered among the "young 'uns" who are bound to push ahead, if they but keep glacial heads to withstand the rackets and temptations of professional life. The Hibernian Mongolian, Charley McCarthy, can use Chinese "guff" with the volubility of a Pekin hoodlum, which is as surprising to the audience as it is to the Boss John of the laundry warerooms and the guileless shirt-wrestling heathen who assist him. J. E. Murphy's Hibernian female in the "Flats," who plays "croquette" and wishes to be "conjaynial.," is as successful in its way as the renowned "Widow O'Brien;" while his active Irishman, with decided vocal and terpsichorean tendencies, who permeates through the "Dream," the "Christening," the "Wedding," etc., is widely known and appreciated.

That you may all get a telegraphic "All right" in answer to every application for dates, that your poor trunks may experience a comfortable non-interruption of travel by reason of wild landlords, and that you may ever find a glorious absence of "low-forehead" audiences, "kranky" managers, bull-headed leaders and accordion orchestras, are the "schemes" I wish you all.

[*New York Clipper*, February 14, 1885]

INDEX

ABOUT WILLIAM L. SLOUT

WILLIAM L. SLOUT recently retired from his position as Professor of Theatre Arts at California State University, San Bernardino. Before embarking on his twenty-four-year academic career, Slout was a working thespian and trooper in circus tent shows, on live television, in commercials, in summer stock theatres across the country, as well as in off-Broadway houses in New York. Following a stint in the Army in World War II, Slout earned a bachelor's degree from Michigan State University in 1949. After completing his master's degree at Utah State University in 1953, he moved to New York, where he met his wife-to-be, Marte, also an actor, and where he appeared in such notable television series productions as *The Kraft Theater* and *Playhouse 90*. Slout moved to Los Angeles in the late 1960s, and received his Ph.D. in Theatre History from the University of California, Los Angeles. He began teaching at Cal State, San Bernardino in 1968, and since then has written and/or edited a variety of books on the history of American theatre. As editor of the Borgo Press series, Clipper Studies in the Theatre, Slout has edited and compiled such titles as *The Theatrical Rambles of Mr. and Mrs. Greene* (1987), *An Annotated Narrative of Joe Blackburn's A Clown's Log* (1993), *Broadway Below the Sidewalk* (1994), *Amphitheatres and Circuses* (1994), *Ink from a Circus Press Agent* (1995), all published by The Borgo Press. His play, *The Trial of Dr. Jekyll*—a sequel to the Stevenson classic—was produced by the Theatre Department at California State University, San Bernardino, in 1993, and published by Borgo the same year. Although now officially retired and living in San Bernardino, he and Marte are often seen at a variety of local theatrical productions, both on the Cal State campus and throughout Southern California.